AN ADVENTURE INTO DISCOVERY

by
Dr. Rex D. Edwards

www.TEACHServices.com • (800) 367-1844

World rights reserved. This book or any portion thereof may not be copied or reproduced in any form or manner whatever, except as provided by law, without the written permission of the publisher, except by a reviewer who may quote brief passages in a review.

The author assumes full responsibility for the accuracy of all facts and quotations as cited in this book. The opinions expressed in this book are the author's personal views and interpretations, and do not necessarily reflect those of the publisher.

This book is provided with the understanding that the publisher is not engaged in giving spiritual, legal, medical, or other professional advice. If authoritative advice is needed, the reader should seek the counsel of a competent professional.

Copyright © 2010 TEACH Services, Inc.
ISBN-13: 978-1-457258-613-0 (Paperback)
Library of Congress Control Number: 2010921429

CONTENTS

Preface .... *v*

Acknowledgments .... *vii*

1. Voices From the Signposts of Antiquity 1
2. Parchments and Jars from "Down Under" 12
3. Apollo and the Other "Gods" or Jesus? 23
4. Gods of Gold and Graves of Ashes 37
5. Secrets in Stone 52
6. Red Stairs to the Sun 67
7. The Strange Fate of Masada 83
8. Encounter at Sinai 95
9. A Statue for Remembrance 113
10. Hoaxed at the Krak des Chevaliers 128
11. Book of the Dead or Word of Life 147
12. The Last Days of Pompeii 163
13. The Golden Age; A New Beginning 177

Endnotes *191*

PREFACE

"But what am I?
An infant crying in the night?
An infant crying for the light?
And with no language but a cry!"
—Alfred L. Tennyson

The churchman intoned the prescribed litany: "Dust to dust..." The grave received the 38-year-old casualty into its yawning mouth. Another mortal has been seized by the orders of omnipotent death. The young mother, widowed by a cruel fate, clutches more tightly to the little bundle imprisoned in her arms, a three-month old daughter never to know her father, while flanking both her sides are her six sons with stinging tears no longer restrained. They would never know what it was to hear a father say, "I am proud of you, son!"

"An infant crying in the night?"—a cry heard in all places and in all ages—a search for meaning in a universe that appears insane, unfair and at the mercy of a mere caprice. And the cry has many styles, to wit:

"Ah, fate, could you and I with him aspire
To grasp this sorry scheme of things entire
Would we not shatter it to bits
And remould it to the heart's desire!"

Was Barbara Tuchman right when she wrote of history as "the unfolding of miscalculation"? As the second eldest of those six boys, I am now of the firm conviction that history is "HIS-story"—the saga of a great, good God whose incredible activities can be traced on the backdrop of man's measurable history. And that "behind, above, and through all the play and counterplay of human interests and power and passions, the agencies of the all-merciful One, silently, patiently working out the counsels of His own will."[1]

But can dusty history educate us? Since history repre-sents the human experience in its totality, it cannot be al-together without value. True, we can neither obtain from the past definitive and detailed directives for a future course of action, nor can we produce from it the ready-made solutions that man desires, but it can nevertheless warn and advise.

What we need as we begin this ADVENTURE INTO DISCOVERY is the right perspective, for common sense has been well expressed in the dictum "he who fails to learn the lessons of history is condemned to repeat its mistakes."

Within the restricted frame of this small volume is an attempt to bring you the assurance that what God made, He governs, and He who controls the cosmos and guides the atom, also desires to share Himself with us and pre-pare us for everlasting togetherness.

Some books are written to answer one's own questions; other books are written to question answers already given. This book was written for both those reasons, and another: to find solace in a God who still intervenes in hu-man life. What I share I owe to others. I therefore claim neither originality nor finality, for as Will Durant writes:

> "Always, in these hurried pages, conscience runs a race with time, and warns the hurrying pen that, like the hasty traveler, it is but scratching the surface. How many publishers, teachers, scholars, patrons, poets, romancers, and reckless rebels labored for half a century to produce the literature that here has been so narrowly confined, so many masterpieces unnamed, nations ignored, once immortal geniuses slighted with a line! It cannot be helped. The ink runs dry."[2]

ACKNOWLEDGMENTS

The author wishes to acknowledge the assistance of Dr. Lawrence Geraty, President Emeritus of La Sierra University and internationally-known authority in Biblical Archaeology and Dr. Gerhard Pfandl, Old Testament scholar for their careful technical editing on matters of historic and biblical accuracy.

I
VOICES FROM THE SIGNPOSTS OF ANTIQUITY

"Out of the monuments, names, words, proverbs, traditions, private records and evidences, fragments of stories, passages of books, and the like, we do save and recover somewhat from the deluge of time."—Francis Bacon

The Italian epigraphist Giovanni Pettinato was baffled. "I cannot understand a single word!" He scrutinized the two rounded objects more carefully. The wedge-shaped signs were certainly ordinary cuneiform. It was not Akkadian. Neither was it Sumerian, the earliest known written Mesopotamian language. It was a new tongue!

As I stood on top of a hill in the blazing sun of northern Syria and watched the archaeologists and their staff digging up the secrets of a little-known kingdom that existed before the days of Abraham, I recalled with a new stir of excitement the time the discovery was first made.

It was back in 1963 when Paola Matthiae, a professor from the University of Rome, was digging into a huge 140-acre mound some 34 miles southwest of Aleppo, now called Tell Mardikh. All at once a large sculptured basin and some pottery were surfaced that convinced him that somewhere below a rich and sophisticated society had once thrived. He was right. Within the next few years he orchestrated an archaeological resurrection as a massive city gate, a royal palace and a large temple were awakened from their 4,300-year slumber.

But who were these people who had lived and loved there? The answer soon came. One day in 1968 diggers pulled from the debris archaeological ore: the broken torso of a royal statue. On its shoulder and chest could be seen the wedge-shaped slashes of history's first-known writing, "cuneiform" (from Latin *cuneus*, wedge). The 26

An Adventure into Discovery

lines were quickly deciphered and on the seventh line appeared the words, "in EBLA." The team members gasped. Could this be the mysterious Ebla mentioned in inscriptions found in Mesopotamia and Egypt? The Italians searched on doggedly for more evidence. In 1973 they began to find ruins at a deeper and, therefore, older level. Pottery fragments—painstakingly dug out, sorted, washed and catalogued—showed that the older city dated back to at least 2400 B.C. Then came the clay tablets, thousands of them scattered on the floor in a room adjoining the excavated palace entrance. Then, just when the digging season was almost over, workmen in another room discovered the find of a lifetime: some 14,000 inscribed tablets, stacked on the floor where they had fallen from burning shelves, most of them intact.

Included in the new find was the vital key to unlock the door to Professor Pettinato's puzzle: more than 100 clay "dictionaries" giving the Sumerian equivalents for the strange words. He could now decipher their meaning; and what a story was surfaced. A hitherto unknown power that ruled in the Near East for a part of the third millennium B.C., of which Ebla was the capital city.

Ebla was obviously a city absorbed with commerce. Many of the clay tablets are "bills of lading," listing cargoes dispatched on donkey caravans. Ebla's weavers and metal workers were farmers, and its artisans exported graceful wooden furniture, overlaid with gold. For these valued products, Ebla's clients may have paid in silver ingots or with such a commodity as barley. Barley provided the city's staple food.

The tablets reflect a sophisticated system of keeping records. Besides renditions of treaties and trade agreements between Ebla and city states in the regions, they include texts on Ebla's polytheistic religion. Some 500 gods and goddesses were worshiped at Ebla, including the familiar Ishtar and Dagan. The tablets also reveal much about Eblan life and customs, including that one king had 38 sons and that the penalty for raping a virgin was death. Other clay tablets in the archives are lessons on examinations for the scribes' school. Kings might issue decrees and merchants negotiate prices, but scribes—key men in Ebla's society—had to translate these decisions into a language understood by all. Month after month, students copied lines written by the teacher in Eblaite and Sumerian. Many tablets have tick marks beside the pupils' errors. Collectively, they paint a picture of a powerful Semitic civilization that reached from the Red Sea to Turkey and east to Mesopotamia.

Among the most tantalizing of Ebla's enigmas are the apparent similarities between some of its tablets and passages of the Old Testament. The tablets contain accounts of a creation and a flood. They mention two cities whose names may be connected to the biblical "sin cities" of Sodom and Gomorrah. The tablets refer to a place called URUSALIMA, clearly Ebla's name for Jerusalem. They make frequent mention of EBRIUM or EBER, possibly identified in the *Book of Genesis* (Gen. 10:21) as the great-great-great-great grandfather of the patriarch, Abraham.

On my last evening at Tell Mardikh, the sky a brilliant tiara of stars, I stood gazing toward the huge mound looming before me, speculating on the mysteries of the past and remembering the testimony of the renowned Jewish archaeologist, Nelson Glueck, who wrote "It may be stated categorically that no archaeological discovery has ever controverted a biblical reference."[4]

What an adventure into certainty it has been to examine the evidence for the historicity of the Biblical text that has come from the spade of the archaeologist. In an older generation it was an accepted axiom that "Dead Men Tell NO Tales!", but our generation knows different. By means of an archaeological resurrection, the great men of antiquity are with us again. From as far distant as 5,000 years they have returned to tell their tales of splendid civilizations, great conquests and cruel customs. The tongueless tombs of the distant past have suddenly become vocal, and this mighty chorus of the dead great, tell

An Adventure into Discovery

tales in a multitude of languages—Egyptian, Sumerian, Babylonian, Hittite and Hebrew. The entire libraries of kings, the correspondence files of important people, the records of business transactions, giant inscriptions and clay tablets stored in museums all over the world enable us to study the evidence that accredits the accuracy of the Biblical story. These are signposts of antiquity that bring to the modern world a voice of certainty.

Two discoveries in particular are of vital importance when it comes to interpreting these signposts. Unless the records of the past can be deciphered, the value of the finds is not perceived. These two finds are the Rosetta Stone and the Behistun Rock.

The first discovery was in a sense the result of political ambition. It is Paris in 1798. The Palace of Versailles had already stood, at least in part, for a century and a half. The famed Eiffel Tower would not be erected for another ninety years. Napoleon Bonaparte had returned from his Italian campaign. He was yet to sweep across Europe, but first his eyes turned towards the East. He wrote:

> "Paris weighs me down like a cloak of lead! This Europe of ours is a molehill. Only in the East, where 600 million human beings live, is it possible to found great empires and realize great revolutions."

And so it was, on May 19, 1798, Napoleon, with 328 vessels and 38,000 men—including 120 scholars and artists—set sail for the land of the Pharaohs. On July 2, they landed on Egyptian soil. Accompanied by 23 of his officers and riding ahead on a swan-white horse, he paused before the great pyramid of Giza and cried, "Soldiers, forty centuries of history are looking down upon you." However, the raid on Egypt was, at least from a military standpoint, ill-advised. His failure was captured in a caricature published in England in 1815. Napoleon was represented as fleeing from Egypt under the enigmatic stare of an oversized Sphinx. The following verse accompanied the cartoon:

Voices From the Signposts of Antiquity

*"The cunning he displayed in the fight,
He manifested in his flight."*

To the verse was attached a moral lesson,

*"Whoe'er attempt t'improve his lot
May lose the whole that he has got;
For speculation and ambition
Oft leave a man in low condition."*

The French held the land of Egypt for a short time, but there was a single event that occurred on this expedition that was to have a long-range effect. In mid-July 1799, the French army engineer Captain Pierre-François Bouchard, while guiding construction work at Fort Julien near the Egyptian port city of Rashied (Rosetta), found a strange stone. The stone was granite, black in color, described as three feet nine inches in height, two feet four and one-half inches in width, and eleven inches thick. The upper portion and lower right corners were broken off.

On a recent visit to the British Museum I again examined the stone. The inscription in three registers, one above the other, is still clear and decipherable. The language in the lower register was the Greek, which could be easily read, but the two other languages were not known to any living persons. The language in the upper register was just like that seen on temple ruins everywhere in Egypt, but was meaningless, as none could read it.

For years various scholars attempted to decipher the two unknown languages, but without avail. The reading of the Greek register disclosed the fact that the stone was a monument set up by some priests about 195 B.C. in honor of Ptolemy V, their ruler, for having canceled certain priestly taxes and having restored the priests to their places in the temple. But the reading of the Greek lines was of little consequence and unlocked no door to the secrets which lay beneath ruins scattered across Egypt's land. It was the language in the upper register of the Ro-

An Adventure into Discovery

setta Stone which had to be deciphered before that bolted door would be unlocked.

The Rosetta Stone
(Courtesy of British Museum)

Then in 1818 the distinguished French Egyptologist, Jean Francois Champollion, came to the task. His record was impressive. At the age of 16 he read before a prestigious French academy a paper in which he maintained that Coptic was the ancient language of Egypt. Later, by the appointment of Charles X, he became director of the Egyptian museum at the Louvre. He was fully aware of the challenge of finding the key to a language that was represented by 750 common figures and 3,500 not so common ones; but a happy thought occurred to him. Perhaps what was written in the lower register in Greek was written in the upper registers in the strange languages. Proceeding upon that assumption, Champollion labored long and arduously to decipher the unknown languages. Using the known Greek as a basis, he deciphered the two other languages and within four years announced his discovery to the world.

The results of the decipherment of the Rosetta Stone were far-reaching. It was found that the inscription in the upper register was the hieroglyphic Egyptian (ancient picture writing), and that the writing in the middle register was demotic Egyptian (a conventionalized picture language developed from the hieroglyphic). What was written upon that stone was of little consequence or interest; but the arrangement made possible the deciphering of the language of the ancient inscriptions, thus unlocking that old civilization to living men. Then the inscriptions on temple walls, in tombs, and everywhere in

Voices From the Signposts of Antiquity

Egypt could be read. It only remained for man to excavate, explore, and translate.

Within a few decades Egypt was the scene of much activity. Explorers were at work digging out the ruins, and scholars were deciphering the inscriptions. A history of Egypt has been constructed. Many of the statements of the Bible, the only book which reached back to that day, have been corroborated by these silent witnesses and signposts of the long ago. The year 1822 marks the birthday of Biblical archaeology.

Close on the heels of the deciphering of the Rosetta Stone was another discovery of major importance. This time it was a real signpost on a public highway.

It was in 1838. An English army officer, Henry C. Rawlinson, on duty in Persia, was crossing the Zagros Mountains on an old caravan route that stretched between Teheran and Baghdad. Cresting the 1700-foot summit, suddenly rounding a bend in the road, his eye was captured by an enormous ancient "signboard" carved into the flattened and smoothed limestone surface. Below the inscription was a large spring, where it is said that every caravan and army that passed from Persia to Babylonia drank. The architect, whoever he was, was obviously a shrewd advertiser.

As it turned out, the inscription was a chronicle of the achievements of Darius I, a Persian king who lived a little more than 500 years before Christ. This "signpost" was more than 2,400 years old. Upon discovering it, Mr. Rawlinson began to sense the possible importance of the inscription. He determined to copy it, with a view to its translation. It proved to be a heroic endeavor because of the inaccessibility of the inscription. It was set about 500 feet from the base of the cliff, and, a fearful chasm of approximately 350 feet deep yawned beneath it. Immediately below the inscription, there was a ledge of rock about fourteen inches wide; but parts of the edges of this ledge had crumbled away as a result of erosion, making its use extremely dangerous; but Rawlinson was undeterred. Assisted by a native, he would stand upon the ledge; sometimes he would work upon a ladder, the base of which rested upon the crumbling ledge. At other times he was suspended in a swing before the columns of writing he was copying. Various schemes were devised, until after four years of courageous effort, painstaking labor, and hazards of such fearful character that few would have been willing to brave them, the task was finally completed.

And what was this ancient "signpost?" There were nine panels: five in the Persian language, three proved to be Median, while the final one was in ancient Babylonian. At the upper right corner there is a panel containing a picture of Darius receiving homage from a group of military captives who have ropes about their necks. The writing was found to be cuneiform, or wedge-shaped characters, making all the columns difficult to read. It was not until the year 1857, twenty-two years after its discovery, that Mr. Rawlinson completed the translation.

The contents of the inscription were of comparatively little interest, being records of military achievements of Darius I, king of Persia. Their interest and value consisted in the fact that the deciphering enabled scholars to read the other ancient records of the civilization of the Euphrates and Tigris Valleys, present-day Iraq. It was, indeed, the key which unlocked the history of the very ancient peoples, apart from which we would have no knowledge of them except through incidental references in the Old Testament.

The exciting aspect of this discovery consists in the fact that it made possible the reconstruction of an Assyrian and Babylonian history, corroborating many references made to these people in the Old Testament. As there was no history, apart from the Bible, which dated back farther than four hundred years before Christ, critics took the liberty to question and even dispute the statement made in the Bible concerning these nations.

Voices From the Signposts of Antiquity

Now all this has changed. The decipherment of these cuneiform "signposts" verifies specific biblical historical data. Need I mention, particularly, that the book of Daniel has found itself in the critics' "den" on more than one occasion? As recently as fifty years ago, many scholars considered Belshazzar, for instance, to be a pure invention on the part of the writer of Daniel 5, because he was unknown from classical sources that discussed in detail that period of Babylonian history; but along came an archaeologist who dug up a whole series of tablets and cylinders to illustrate that Belshazzar was, indeed, the last ruler of Babylon. In fact, he was co-regent, and sat on the throne with his father, Nabonidus, who alone was remembered in classical sources.

Much more has come from the ruins of Babylon. As I stood among those mud bricks, all that remains of that once great Mesopotamian city, I saw Nebuchadnezzar's name inscribed in cuneiform. I remembered it was here that a record of Jehoiachin's Babylonian captivity was found, and the famous "Babylonian Chronicles," which mentions King Zedekiah, was unearthed.

Not the least among the literature of Assyria was the great library of Ashurbanipal of Nineveh, with its 26,000 "volumes"—not volumes as we know them, but volumes of clay tablets, cones, and cylinders, discovered by local native, Hormuzd Rassam, in 1854.

From Assyrian records we have Israelite kings that are named. We even have a picture of Jehu, the Israelite king, kneeling before King Shalmaneser III, the Assyrian king, on the so-called "black obelisk." This impressive four-sided six and one-half foot high "signpost" was set up in the center of Shalmaneser's sixteen-square mile city. Archaeology has recently provided confirmation of each one of Nehemiah's enemies mentioned there in that Biblical book. It has given us abundant evidence of the existence of the Assyrian king, Sargon. In 1963, a "signpost" that he set up in Ashdod, right on the coast of Palestine, was found, and this corroborated the very specific statement concerning Sargon's presence in Ashdod that we read about in Isaiah 20:1. (Similarly, a cuneiform inscribed prism corroborates Sennacherib's unsuccessful siege of Jerusalem in the days of Isaiah, recorded in Isaiah 36 and 37.)

Were it not for the Behistun key, providentially discovered and painstakingly deciphered, we would be ignorant of the context in which the Bible story took place. You see, archaeology has illustrated scores of Biblical customs and practices. For instance, it has shown that Abraham's relationship with Sarah and Hagar was in accordance with the practice of the times. Clay tablets inscribing similar incidents have been recovered from the Mesopotamian city of Nusi. They date back to the middle of the second millennia B.C., roughly the time of the patriarchs. A barren wife was expected to arrange for her husband to have a child by a suitable slave girl. All these laws were inscribed in cuneiform. The slave girls' economic security was assured, and their offspring became the legal heir, unless the true wife bore a child. Another Nusi tablet tells of a man who sold his birthright for three sheep. The transaction is recorded right there for us to read, and we are reminded of Esau selling Jacob his right as the firstborn. As already mentioned, the dramatic new finds at Ebla, in Syria, promise further elucidation on this period, the patriarchal period of Biblical history.

So without the Behistun key, the voices which now speak out from the mounds and dust heaps of ancient Babylonia and Assyria would be as silent as they had been for more than two millenniums.

Dr. James Orr reflected:

> "Nothing in the whole course of the past century is more remarkable than the recovery of the knowledge of ancient civilization through the labors of explorers, and the successful decipherment of old inscriptions. It must be accounted a wonderful providence of God that, at a time when so much has been said and done to discredit the Old Testament, so marvelous a series of

discoveries, bearing directly on matters contained in its pages, should have been made."

What can these "signposts" teach us? In answering this question, Old Testament scholar and archaeologist Professor Lawrence Geraty states,

> "Firstly, that the discoveries of archaeology are really Providential in nature, and it's an exciting time to be alive and to see Providence at work.
>
> "Secondly, these "signposts" illuminate the world of the Bible, but they cannot establish its claim to a truth of a higher order. The truth of the Bible is of a spiritual order that can neither be proven nor contradicted. It can't be confirmed or invalidated by material discoveries—the things that we can touch and feel, that archaeologists tend to find. Archaeology can bring understanding, but rarely does it create faith. The authority and trustworthiness of Biblical truths require a commitment of faith. Faith is the gift of God, which comes to those who ask for it. If we come to the Bible without faith, we will find only interesting historical religious documents in Scripture; but to the believer, the Bible will become God's living Word, ministering to his needs today. As we examine these "signposts" and the archaeological data, we will be encouraged to know that our Bible is not simply a patchwork of legends, but rather remarkably reliable records of men and women, who, themselves, have responded to the revelation of God in history."

"Seek ye out the Book of the Lord, and read: no one of these shall fail." Isaiah 34:16.

II
PARCHMENTS AND JARS FROM "DOWN UNDER"

"Tradition has dug for it a grave;
Intolerance has lighted for it many a fagot;
Many a Judas has betrayed it with a kiss;
Many a Peter has denied it with an oath;
Many a Demas has forsaken it;
  But the Word of God still endures."

It was the year 1547. Edward VI was receiving the crown of the British Empire in Westminster Abbey. He was presented with three swords, symbols of his sovereignty over England, Ireland and France. Can you imagine the astonishment of his chamberlains, when the king suddenly called for a fourth sword! Was there another? Who could have made such a bungle in the coronation preparations? The king resolved their fear and embarrassment when he asked for a Bible which he identified as "the sword of the Spirit, which is the Word of God." Thus the Bible was carried before him in the coronation procession, a custom that is still observed when the sovereigns of England are crowned. In fact, when her gracious majesty, Elizabeth II was crowned on June 2, 1953, I remember the Archbishop of Canterbury, when presenting the Bible to the Queen, saying: "We present you with this book, the most valuable thing in all the world."

Is it valuable? Perhaps values are best appreciated by comparison. A first Folio Edition of the words of William Shakespeare brought $83,965 at a sale in Hamburg, Germany. By contrast, a copy of the book of Revelation, believed to have been copied and illuminated about A.D. 1250 in the Benedictine Abbey of St. Albans, England, sold to a wealthy New Yorker for $182,000. Nor to mention a Gutenberg Bible—one of the remaining 47 of the original 185 still surviving—that sold to a bookseller for two million dollars. Apparently the General Theological

Parchments and Jars from "Down Under"

Seminary of New York City had come on hard times and decided to auction its copy! These rare Gutenberg Bibles (Latin Text) are reputed to be the most expensive in the world.

The Bible is valuable, but it is also very popular. While the works of Shakespeare have been translated into 35 languages, and Bunyan's *Pilgrim's Progress* into 40 languages, according to the Wycliffe Bible Translators, the Bible, in whole or in part, is presently available in no less than 2,261 languages and dialects.

Yet, paradoxically, despite its value and popularity, no other book has ever had such a battle to fight as the Bible. It has had to brave the trampling and crushing of the ages. Critics, atheists, and the unholy have made war upon it. Condemned, outlawed, burned, buried, and forbidden to the sons of men, it has warred a great warfare against the pride and destructive elements of human life; but it has swung over the ages in a deathless existence that has mocked the very powers that sought to extinguish its sacred flame.

In 1778 the caustic French skeptic, Voltaire, declared that the Bible, within 100 years of his day, would be an extinct relic found only in museums. Today, the very place where he made that boast is now a Bible-producing book room in the city of Paris! The book is valuable, popular, and seems to be indestructible. Did not St. Peter, the big fisherman, describe it as "the Word of God...that liveth and abideth forever" (I Peter 1:23)? The very failure of man to expunge the sacred page is evidence of the remarkable way that Providence has superintended its transmission from age to age.

Is it accurate? People continue to ask, "How do you know that the Bible from which you read today is anything like that which the authors, back in the time of the prophets, penned?" Up until the age of archaeology, the Christian had to answer, "Well, by faith, I believe that the Lord has preserved a Bible that is essentially the same

An Adventure into Discovery

as the authors who wrote it down." It was a matter of "faith," not proof...but today we have the evidence.

It is the early spring of 1947. A thin, dark-faced Bedouin boy of 15, rejoicing in the exotic name of Muhammed the Wolf, was minding some goats near a cliff on the western shore of the Dead Sea. He belonged to a party of shepherd boys who were smuggling their goats and other goods out of Transjordania into Palestine. They were on their way to Bethlehem to sell their stuff on the black market, and they had detoured as far south as the Dead Sea for two reasons: firstly, to circumvent the heavily-guarded customs gate on the Jordan Bridge, and secondly, to stock up with water at the spring of Ain Feshkha, the only fresh water to be found for miles in that dry, hot and desolate region.

One of the goats strayed away, and the goatherd was forced to climb up the cliffside to retrieve it. For some reason he flung a stone into a cave about his head—some say it was in the process of his search for the wandering goat, others that it was no more than the idle tossing of a stone into an inviting opening. The significant thing is that he did it.

How startled he was when his stone-pitching ploy was immediately followed by the unmistakable clank of something breaking in the depths of the cave. Anyone who recalls a childhood incident featuring a ball and a broken window will know fairly accurately how that shepherd lad felt, and will not be surprised at his reaction. He ran away!

It was not long before his courage returned and he came back to investigate, bringing another lad for company. The two boys scaled up the cliff face, squeezed through the narrow opening, lowered themselves to the floor of the cave, which measured about six feet wide and twenty-six feet long. They peered into the dimness. Here among bits of pottery they found several tan cylindrical jars about two feet in height. Tearing off their bowl-like lids, the boys reached down inside and extracted, instead of gold and gems, some dark, foul-smelling lumps wrapped in linen. They carried them out into the sunlight, jerked the linen loose and stared sadly at three scrolls coated with a black substance resembling pitch. It was actually decomposed leather.

The Qumran Dead Sea Caves

The scrolls were from three to twenty-four feet long, made of cardboard-thin sheepskin leather sewn together. On one side were columns of strange writing—an archaic form of Hebrew. The boys were deeply disappointed. Little did these lads realize that in their unsuspecting hands they held one of the most sensational discoveries and fantastic finds of the twentieth century, the Dead Sea Scrolls.

The boys continued their journey to Bethlehem, disposed of their contraband goods, and offered the larger of the scrolls to an antiquities dealer for the diminutive sum of $40. He turned them down, never dreaming that in a few years, five of the original find of eleven scrolls would sell for the astronomical sum of $220,000. Today those manuscripts are priceless.

An interesting question emerges. Why did the boys retain possession of the parchments when they were told that the scrolls were "worthless?" Their answer: "The scrolls are made of leather. If we cut them up into thin strips they will make very good sandal straps!" Who can doubt that a happy Providence was very much involved in the final destination of those "worthless" parchments! Subsequent events prove it.

Since 1947, 230 caves in the same region have been carefully searched, many of which have yielded a veri-

An Adventure into Discovery

table harvest of precious documents and pottery remains dating back before the days of Christ.

Why had such a valuable library been deposited in this desolate, uninviting, desert wilderness? The answer lay less than 600 yards from the caves, in some ruins which had been located on maps for decades. In 1952-55, archaeologists began to dig in these stone ruins, called Khirbet Qumran. As they dug, they uncovered the fabulous history of an ancient community known as the Essenes, and discovered why the precious scrolls had been hidden in the cliff caves. It all began in Jerusalem before Christ was born.

Archaeological evidence shows that about 135 B.C., conflict arose between the spiritual leaders of Judaism and a pietistic sect called the Essenes. The reformers moved into the wilderness. Their "teacher" and his followers found at Qumran the remains of King Uzziah's eighth-century B.C. military outpost known as the "City of Salt" and built a monastery on the spot. It is 1,000 feet below sea level, comfortably warm in winter but an inferno of heat in the summer. Notwithstanding the discomfiture of their new environment, the desert was more to be desired than the inhospitality of Jerusalem. The Essenes could now lead a life of prayer and meditation in peace. They embraced a discipline as unyielding as their mountain stronghold. Their way of life was expressed in a manuscript found at Qumran caned "A Manual of Discipline," part of which reads:

> "And this is the rule for the men of the community who freely have pledged themselves to be converted from all evil and to cling to all of his commandments according to his will."

They read the Scriptures continuously by dividing themselves into shifts. Their favorite books were Deuteronomy, Isaiah, Psalms, and Daniel.

As archaeologists continued their excavations, they uncovered a large building called a Scriptorium, contain-

Parchments and Jars from "Down Under"

ing a writing room. While Qumran, as a single place, has produced 600 mss with 500 different handwriting styles, clearly the Scriptorium was the place where the scribes were taught the ancient art. They had stumbled upon the place in which the scribes were taught the ancient art; also found were the remains of a long table resting on pedestals, and some inkpots, one even containing dried ink. A complete jar was found which was identical with those found in the cave. Clearly, the Essenes must have written their precious parchments there, but when did this happen? The discovery of over 400 coins, none of which were dated later than A.D. 68, gave the scholars a clue.

About A.D. 66 a tide of nationalism swept across Judaism. With a mighty surge, the Jews attempted once and for all to break the Roman yoke that held them like a vise. The Jews did not have a reputation of being a cooperative subject race. Their Roman masters said, "Enough!" The tenth legion was marched into the land of Palestine. Every pocket of resistance was put down. No mercy was shown. The Essenes tucked away in desert isolation were not sheltered from the storm. Warned of the approach of the legionnaires, they concealed their library and fled.

Today most of the scrolls from Qumran are housed in a place in Jerusalem called the *Shrine of the Book*. Its shining white dome, made in the likeness of the lid

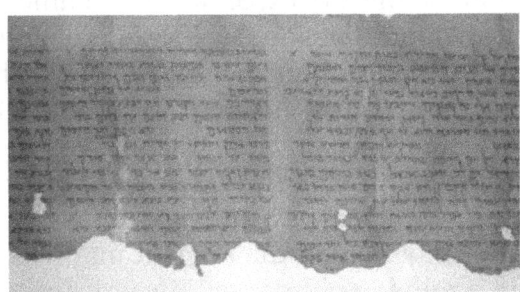

The Isaiah Scroll

of a Dead Sea Scroll jar, stands out impressively on the Israel Museum Compound; but what is on the inside is even more impressive: a copy of an Isaiah school, complete with the 66 chapters set out on 17 sheepskins all sewn together, predating the birth of Jesus by at least 150 years, and some of the oldest fragments ever found, in-

17

cluding a fragment from the book of Exodus that dates to the last half of the third century B.C.

Why was this find at Qumran greeted with such excitement by Biblical scholars?

It must be understood that before 1947, no ancient Hebrew Bible manuscripts had been discovered older than the ninth century of the Christian Era, with the exception of the *Nash Papyrus*, a little fragment containing the Decalogue and a short quotation from Deuteronomy. This document, coming from the first century B.C., was the only direct witness of the Hebrew Old Testament earlier than the Masoretic manuscripts of a much later date.

It is true that a number of manuscripts of the Septuagint, the famous Greek translation of the Old Testament, have been found during the last century and a half, among them the well-known *Codex Sinaiticus* of the fourth century, discovered by Tischendorf in 1844; the *Chester Beatty Papyri* in 1931 containing manuscripts of several Old Testament books of the second and third centuries A.D.; and a few scraps of two pre-Christian copies of the book of Deuteronomy. All these manuscripts, with the exception of the *Codex Sinaiticus*, came from Egypt, whose dry climate has marvelously preserved perishable material. However, no ancient Hebrew Bible manuscripts had ever turned up in any place, and Old Testament scholars, therefore, had given up hope long ago of ever finding Hebrew manuscripts that were older than those already known. Such pessimism was best expressed by the author of a text on the ancient manuscripts which I studied in a religion class over 25 years ago, the then internationally-famous Biblical scholar, Sir Frederick Kenyon, who wrote:

> "There is, indeed, no probability that we shall ever find manuscripts of the Hebrew text going back to a period before the formation of the text which we know as Masoretic."

Parchments and Jars from "Down Under"

The reasons for the absence of ancient Hebrew manuscripts were twofold: (1) The Jewish wars of the first and second centuries and the ensuing persecutions of Jews in many lands, causing the destruction of the old Jewish literature; and (2) an old Jewish regulation that worn-out Bible manuscripts were sacred, since they contained the name of God, and whenever one was worn-out, or its reading became illegible, it was placed in a receptacle in the synagogue called a "Genizah." Such a genizah might only be a box in a small synagogue or a room in a larger one. Whenever a prominent member of the synagogue died, one of these discarded Bible rolls was put in his coffin, and in this way disintegrated and was lost forever.

For these two reasons, the Jewish wars and persecutions, and the practice of discarding old Bible manuscripts, none of the famous Hebrew books of the time of Christ, or the early centuries of the Christian era, survived. But then, with the discovery of the Dead Sea Scrolls, suddenly and Providentially, scholars actually had in their hands documents that took them 1,000 years closer to the original text.

However, it is further argued, "We still don't have any of the original Hebrew manuscripts. How do we know that copies were accurate?" Well, the accuracy of copies made from the original was guaranteed by two very remarkable characteristics of Hebrew life. Firstly, the Hebrew language experienced very few changes throughout the entire period of its written history. This is not true of the English language. Compare, for instance, the Anglo-Saxon Chronicles (A.D. 700-1100) with a page from Chaucer (ca. 1400), and then in turn read a Shakespearean play (ca. 1616) and compare it with a poem from Tennyson (ca. 1892). You will find that Anglo-Saxon is quite unintelligible; Chaucer would be readable with a little practice; Shakespeare would be found to contain many archaisms; but Tennyson would be read with ease. English has experienced an enormous evolution in the character of the letters, and both syntax and grammar; but there was no such development in the Hebrew language. It shows fixity and uniformity through the whole period in which the Old Testament writings were penned. However, understand that, during the Exile, the Hebrew script did change from proto-Hebraic to the square Hebrew letters now used. Notwithstanding, scribes who were copying from the original were never impaired in their work of copying by unfamiliar grammatical forms or unrecognizable characters despite the fact that several Hebrew letters resemble each other.

Secondly, the scholars took exceptional care and meticulous thoroughness to ensure the accuracy of the copy. For instance, three things were done after a scribe had completed a single line, and before he could proceed to the next: he would count the number of words in the line, then the number of letters, and finally fix middle words and letters in that line. Only when he was assured that the copy was identical with the original would he then proceed. Since no mistakes were corrected—because alterations were not permitted—if a mistake was found in the copy, it was destroyed and the laborious handwritten process was begun all over again.

These two factors, then—the fixity and uniformity of the language and the meticulous care of the scribes—ensured accuracy of copies that were made. The Dead Sea Scrolls represent the ultimate test because some of these manuscripts date to within two hundred years of the date of composition. A careful comparison of these documents with the later ones establishes the meticulous care with which these were copied.

Indeed, the Dead Sea Scrolls have completely revolutionized scholars' appreciation for the accuracy of the text. After the minutest examination of 10–15,000 fragments of every book of the Old Testament, with the exception of the book of Esther, scholars have come to the staggering conclusion that the Old Testament text has experienced virtually no change during the past 2,000 years, for the text of the Dead Sea Scrolls is for all practical purposes *identical* with the Hebrew Bible on which *all* modern translations are based.

The greatest authority on Middle East Archaeology up to the time of his death, W. F. Albright, commenting on this find, says, "We may rest assured that the consonantal text of the Hebrew Bible, though not infallible, has been preserved with an accuracy perhaps unparalleled in any other Near- Eastern Literature."[5]

Professor Frank M. Cross, member of the permanent staff working on the Dead Sea Scrolls, says:

> "Not only in Isaiah, but in other prophetic books, indeed, in the entire Old Testament, we must now assume that the Old Testament Text was stabilized early, and that late recessional activities were only of slight effect."[6]

Dr. Millar Burrows, head of Yale University's Department of Near Eastern Languages and Literature, was director of the American School of Oriental Research when the scrolls were discovered. After working intimately with them for years and translating much of the material into English, he testified:

> "There is no danger that our understanding of the Bible will be so revolutionized by the Dead Sea Scrolls as to require a revision of any basic article of the Christian Faith."

What about the New Testament? We have copies of the New Testament books on papyrus dating back to the second or the third centuries after Christ. Like the Hebrew Old Testament manuscripts, after careful comparison between these manuscripts and the Bibles that we hold in our hands, we can conclude that, despite the thousands of textual variants that we know of in the Greek manuscripts of the New Testament (most of which are quite minor), for all practical purposes, the words of the Bible have been transmitted carefully and accurately down through the centuries.

An Adventure into Discovery

The evidence confirms the verdict of the Westminster Assembly theologians, who confessed that the inspired Scriptures were by God's "singular care and Providence kept pure in all ages."

Why has "Providence" superintended an accurate transmission of His Word throughout the ages? Because it is the medium of His voice. Our concern with the Bible, therefore, should be more with its function than with the Bible itself. That is, the God to whom it bears witness should be central in our interest rather than the instrument through which that witness comes. It is not the Bible which speaks, but GOD who speaks through the Bible. To illustrate, the function of a light bulb is to be the medium of producing light. The bulb is not the light, yet you do not have light without the bulb. Its value is that *light comes through it.*

The Bible is the instrument through which God speaks, the means by which His light is cast upon life. If we turn our attention to the Bible itself rather than to the voice, the light, and the God from whom they come, we should be putting the Bible in the place of God, and that voice has been accurately preserved, then we should *listen through it.*

We have the tendency to read books about the Bible rather than to read the Bible itself. Consulting secondary sources does have merit, because the Bible can be a difficult book. We need all the help we can get to understand it. But let not that quest for understanding take the place of coming to the Bible directly, and with patience and determination listening to the voice of God, there; hearing the Word of God which He, Himself, has spoken. And having heard His Word then

> Seize its principles and abide in them;
> Learn its promises and lean on them;
> Ponder its precepts and obey them

for then your quest for certainty will not be in vain.

III
APOLLO AND THE OTHER "GODS" OR JESUS?

"He who was foretold and foreshadowed by the holy religion of Judea, which was designed to free the universal aspiration of in mankind from every impure element, he has come to instruct, to obey, to love, to die, and by dying to save mankind."—Edmond Dehaut de Pressense

The whole of Greece was in an uproar! Xerxes, the Persian Conqueror, with a vast army at his heels, was threatening Europe. Many Greek states had given away before him, sending him offerings of earth and water—tokens of submission. But the Athenians, urged on by their leader, Themistocles, wanted to resist, but first it was necessary to consult the Delphic Oracle. They put the question to the Pythoness—the name of the woman who spoke the God Apollo's Oracles in his temple—whose reply chilled their hearts:

"All...is ruined and lost. Since Fire, and the impetuous Ares,
Speeding along in a Syrian chariot, hastes to destroy her.
Not alone shalt thou suffer: full many the towers he will level
Many the shrines of the gods he will give to fiery destruction.
Even now they stand dark with sweat horribly dripping,
Trembling and quaking with fear: and lo! from the high roof trickleth
Black blood, sign prophetic hard distress impending,
Get away from the temple; and brood on the ill that await ye."

An Adventure into Discovery

HERODOTUS says that when the Athenians received this reply they were at first overcome with grief, but later, on the advice of Timon, the son of Androbolus, they returned carrying olive branches, and entered the sanctuary as supplicants. This time the oracle gave a more soothing response:

> "Then far-seeing Zeus grants this to the prayers of Athene;
> Safe shall the wooden wall continue for thee and they children.
> Wait not the tramp of horse, nor the footmen mightily moving
> Over land, but turn your back on the foe, and retire ye.
> Yet shall the day arrive when ye shall meet him in battle.
> Holy Salamis, thou shalt destroy the offspring of women,
> When men scatter the seed, or when they gather the harvest."

This was Apollo at his most ambiguous. What were the "wooden walls"? And what was the significance of "holy Salamis?" Themistocles had no doubts. He told the assembled elders:

> "Rightly taken, the response of the god threatens the enemy, much more than the Athenians, I counsel you to make ready to fight on board ships. They are the wooden walls in which the gods tell you to trust!"

Themistocles was right! The Athenians evacuated their city, and from the island of Salamis saw the Persians burn their homes and temples; but when they met the enemy in the narrows, the Athenians and their allies put up such a fight that the mighty Persian fleet was boarded, set on fire, and sunk. Xerxes' army was suddenly deprived of naval support. The colossus which had threatened all Europe was brought to a halt. Next year it began to crawl back to Asia, losing thousands by disease and starvation.

Apollo and the Other "Gods" or Jesus?

Athens had saved Greece, and not only Greece but Western Civilization.

Did Themistocles bribe the Delphian Priests to give the answer which he wanted? It is possible, although Herodotus, who had spoken to men who had lived through this period, never once hinted at bribery. Most of the Greeks believed with their poet, Pindar, that:

> "Apollo knows the end supreme of all things, and all the ways that lead thereto; the number of leaves that the earth putteth forth in spring; the number of sands that are in the sea, and the rivers that are driven before the waves and the rushing winds; what is to be, and whence it is to come."

The Temple of Apollo, Delphi

SUCH a claim is rivaled only by the God of the Hebrews of whom it is written: "...I am God, and there is none else: I am God and there is none like me" (Isaiah 26:9). And wherein lies the uniqueness of Israel's God and His claim to preeminence among the pantheon of the gods? The next verse answers the question. "Declaring the end from the beginning, and from ancient times the things that are not yet done...." (v. 10).

An Adventure into Discovery

I had to go to Delphi. So, one sultry spring morning when hill and dale "hangs her infant blossoms on the trees," I left Athens. The coach skirted the base of the Acropolis which in the days of Themistocles formed the center of the city, past monuments hoary with age like the temple of Olympian Zeus with its 16 columns and Hadrian's arch. Out across the plains of Marathon where in the 5th century B.C. the Greeks proved the superiority of their armies over Darius. And who can forget the legend of Pheidippides, the swift runner who ran the 26 miles to Athens announcing the good news, and then dropping dead from exhaustion. Up through the mountains that once echoed with the ring of chariot wheels, the clatter of hooves and the cry of the mortally wounded. Not far is the famous pass of Thermopylae, where in 480 B.C. the Spartans fought against the Persian invaders. For six days, 6,000 Greeks held the 50-foot wide pass, until the treachery of a traitorous comrade betrayed the secret to the enemy and 300 Spartans of the rear guard fell, to a man.

Anticipation mounted as the coach slowly winds up towards the second highest mountain in Hellas—the 8,000-foot-high Mt. Parnassus. Up there, there are only barren cliffs and a screaming wind where the eagles ride, and on a high plateau extending from the base of this mountain is Delphi, adjacent to the village of Kastri. The whole population of this village was moved by the French archaeologists in order to excavate the area where the sanctuary of Delphi was built. On the edge of the village the land plunges down for another 2,000 feet of almost sheer cliffs. There is a steep track here called "the Bad Stair." Up that rocky pathway the Thyriads—ecstatic women who followed Dionysius—clambered on winter nights to the heights above, there to celebrate their sacred rites and dance by the light of torches.

One cannot avoid, of course, the flocks of tourists with Leicas and Nikons clinging to their necks debouching from coaches and squatting on the steps of the Theater, while Greek guides harangue them. We leave the crowd

Apollo and the Other "Gods" or Jesus?

and wander among the columns of Apollo's temple, ascend the steps to the running track and the chariot racing course. Returning, we pass the plinths which once supported statues of Praxiteles, Pheidias and hundreds of others. Below the road we see the circular Temple dedicated to an earth deity, and on past clumps of olives there is the plain of Crisa, and far beyond there is a strip of blue, the Gulf of Corinth.

In spite of the vibrant heat, the air is bracing and pure, scented faintly by the perfume of thyme. You are at Delphi, at the shrine of Apollo; for a thousand years one of the holiest places on Earth.

The story of Delphi and the beginning of the religion of Apollo was recorded by the poet Hesiod some 800 years before Christ, and the legend of how Apollo came to Delphi was probably 1,000 years older. But from the tangle of myths and legends, we catch one interesting thread—that Apollo ruled here and his oracles were spoken by a woman, called the *Pythoness*.

When the Delphic Oracle was at the height of its fame, kings and statesmen, poets and philosophers, and thousands of ordinary people besides came to it from every part of the Greek world and from Asia. The method of consultation, as far as can be ascertained, is this: When the pilgrims consulted the oracle, they had first to wash from the fountain of Castalia and afterwards offer a cake and a victim on the altar in front of the temple. The poor brought a goat or a sheep; the rich, one or more oxen.

The supplicants then handed their questions to the Delphic priest. These questions were not necessarily inquiries into the course of future events. Most of them were requests for guidance. A Greek city, overpopulated, wants to found a new colony; but where? Let us ask Apollo. A Greek state is at war with another, and has laid siege to a certain city. Can it be taken or must the siege be lifted? A statesman wants guidance on policy, or a young man choice of a career.

An Adventure into Discovery

One by one they enter the great pillared temple and eventually are admitted to the *adyton*, the tiny cell in which sits the Pythoness on her tripod. Aromatic herbs are burned before her. The priests stand by, waiting for her replies to the questions. She is always an ordinary woman of no education, and her replies, delivered under the stress of the divine frenzy, are incomprehensible to the supplicants. It is the function of the priests to translate them into verses, but these are not always easy to understand. Frequently they are obscure and double-edged, which was why one of Apollo's names was *Loxias*—the ambiguous!

This was the omniscient Apollo, god of reason, law and justice, whose judgments, as revealed by the Delphic Oracle, were accepted by some of the finest minds of the fifth century B.C. Socrates himself wrote:

> "...does she (the Pythoness) not likewise, from the tripod, declare by a voice, the divine oracles? And truly that god foreknoweth the future; and also showeth it to whomsoever he pleaseth."

Like all polytheistic worship, doomed by Divine Edict—"Thou shalt have no other gods before me!" (Ex. 20:3)—gradually Apollo lost his power. The Romans, coarse, practical, unaesthetic, approached Delphi with curiosity but little reverence. When the Emperor Constantine adopted Christianity as the official religion of the Empire, the reign of the old gods was over. Their temples were deserted, their statues overthrown, and no more offerings were made at their altars. Later, during the reign of Emperor Theodosius (378–395), conversion to Christianity became compulsory.

In the eighth century B.C., Isaiah issued his challenge to the ancient gods:

> "Present your case, says the Lord: bring forward your reasons...let them come near and foretell to what is that shall happen! What are the things of long ago? Tell us, that we may reflect upon them and know their outcome; or declare to us the things to come! Foretell the

Apollo and the Other "Gods" or Jesus?

things that shall come afterward, that we may know that you are gods! Do something, good or evil, that will put us in awe and in fear." —Isaiah 41:21-23, NAB.

And if they had no "case" to "present," then "you are nothing and your work is naught! To choose you is an abomination" (v. 24); and so it was when the last champion of the pagan gods, Julian the Apostate, became Emperor. Like his predecessors he sent ambassadors to Delphi. They came along the ancient road, past neglected statues to gods and heroes already half-forgotten, and presented themselves at the shrine of Apollo, to which for more than a thousand years the greatest rulers of earth had come, humbly with their offerings. But the answer given by the Pythoness brought no comfort to the emperor's ambassadors:

> "Tell the King the fair-wrought hail has fallen to the ground.
> Phoebus has no longer a dwelling, or prophetic laurel,
> Neither has he a speaking fountain;
> The water of speech even is quenched..."

Isaiah's prediction is matched by reality: "You are nothing and your work is naught," for from the village of Kastri, a single bell tolls, calling worshipers of the God who overthrew the statues.

The singular uniqueness of Israel's God was the enduring nature of His Word. Unlike the Delphic Oracle whose "speech even is quenched," the "speech" of God recorded in the writings of the prophets—His spokesmen—still persists. The ultimate validation of that Word is seen in the striking fulfillment of its predictions on the page of history, for "....when the word of the prophet shall come to pass, then shall the prophet be known, that the Lord hath truly sent him" (Jer. 28:9). The fulfillment of such prophecies then stamps the Bible with the very signature of God.

Most remarkable of Old Testament prophecies relate to the appearance of God in the person of Jesus Christ.

An Adventure into Discovery

Of course history is full of men who have claimed that they come from God, or that they were gods, or that they bore messages from God—Buddha, Mohammed, Confucius, Lao-tze, and thousands of others. Each of them has a right to be heard and considered; but a yardstick external to whatever is to be measured is needed. There must be some permanent tests available to all men, all civilizations, and all ages, by which they can decide whether any of these claimants, or all of them, are justified in their claims. These tests are two kinds: reason and history. Reason, because everyone has it, even those without faith; history, because everyone lives in it and should know something about it.

Reason dictates that, if any one of these men actually came from God, the least thing that God could do to support His claim would be to pre-announce His coming. Automobile manufacturers tell their customers when to expect a new model. If God sent anyone from Himself with a vitally important message for all men, it would seem reasonable that He would first let men know when His messenger was coming, where He would be born, where He would live, the doctrine He would teach, the enemies He would make, the program He would adopt for the future, and the manner of His death. By the extent to which the messenger conformed to these announcements, one could judge the validity of his claims.

Reason further assures us that if God did not do this, then there would be nothing to prevent any imposter from appearing in history and saying, "I came from God," or "An angel appeared to me in the desert and gave me this message." In such cases there would be no objective, historical way of testing the messenger. We would have only his word for it.

If a visitor came from a foreign country to Washington and said he was a diplomat, the government would ask him for his passport and other documents testifying that he represented a certain government. His papers would have to antedate his coming. If such proofs of identity are asked from delegates of other countries, reason certainly ought to do so with messengers who claim to have come from God. To each claimant reason says, "What record was there before you were born that you were coming?"

With this test one can evaluate the claimants. Socrates had no one to foretell his birth. Buddha had no one to pre-announce him and his message or tell the day when he would sit under a tree. Confucius did not have the name of his mother and his birthplace recorded, nor were they given to men centuries before he arrived so that when he did come, men would know he was a messenger from God. With Christ it was different. His biography was written before He was born. Because of the Old Testament prophecies, His coming was not unexpected. There were no predictions about Buddha, Confucius, Lao-tze, Mohammed, or anyone else; but there were predictions about Christ. Others just came and said, "Here I am, believe me." They were, therefore, only men and not the Divine in the human. Christ alone stepped out of that line and challenged, "OK! Search the writings of the Jewish people and the related history of the Babylonians, Persians, Greeks, and Romans."

It is true that the prophecies of the Old Testament can be best understood in the light of their fulfillment. The language of prophecy does not have the exactness of mathematics. Yet, if one searches out the various Messianic currents in the Old Testament, and compares the resulting picture with the life and work of Christ, can one doubt that the ancient predictions point to Jesus and the kingdom which He established? God's promise to the patriarchs that through them all the nations of the earth would be blessed; the prediction that the tribe of Judah would be supreme among the other Hebrew tribes until the coming of Him whom all nations would obey; the strange yet undeniable fact that in the Bible of the Alexandrian Jews, the Septuagint, one finds clearly predicted the virgin birth of the Messiah (Isaiah 7:14); the actual location of His birthplace (Micah 5:2); the prophecy of Isaiah 53 about the way Christ would die, the Servant of the Lord, who will lay down His life as a guilt-offering for His people's offenses; the perspectives of the glorious, everlasting kingdom of the House of David—in whom but Christ have these prophecies found their fulfillment? From a historical point of view alone, here is a uniqueness which sets Christ apart from all other founders of world religions; and once that fulfillment of these prophecies did historically take place in the person of Christ, not only did all prophecies cease in Israel, but there was discontinuance of sacrifices when the true Lamb was sacrificed (Daniel 9:26, 27).

Turn to pagan testimony. Tacitus, speaking for the ancient Romans, says, "People were generally persuaded in the faith of the ancient prophecies: that the East was to prevail, and that from Judea was to come the Master and Ruler of the world." Suetonius, in his account of the life of Vespasian, recounts the Roman tradition thus: "It was an old and constant belief throughout the East, that by indubitably certain prophecies, the Jews were to attain the highest power."

China had the same expectation; but because it was on the other side of the world, it believed that the great Wise Man would be born in the West. *The Annals of the Celestial Empire* contain the statement:

> "In the 24th year of the Tchao-Wang of the dynasty of the Tcheou, on the 8th day of the 4th moon, a light appeared in the South-west which illumined the king's palace. The monarch, struck by its splendor, interrogated the sages. They showed him books in which this prodigy signified the appearance of the great Saint of the West whose religion was to be introduced into their country."

When the Delphic Oracle was at its height, the Greeks expected Him, for Aeschylus in his Prometheus six centuries before His coming, wrote: "Look not for any end, moreover, to this curse until God appears, to accept upon His head the pangs of thy own sins vicarious."

How did the Magi of the East know of His coming? Probably from the many prophecies circulated through the world by the Jews as well as through the prophecy made to the Gentiles by Daniel centuries before His birth.

Cicero, after recounting the sayings of the ancient oracles and the Sibyls about a "King whom we must recognize to be saved," asked in expectation, "To what man and to what period of time do these predictions point?" The *Fourth Eclogue* of Virgil recounted the same ancient tradition and spoke of a chaste woman, smiling on her infant boy, with whom the iron age (reference to the Roman Empire, cf. Dan. 2:40; 7:7) would pass away."

Suetonius quoted a contemporary author to the effect that the Romans were so fearful about a king who would rule the world that they ordered any children born that year to be killed—an order that was not fulfilled, except by Herod (cf. Jer. 31:15–17; Matt. 2:16–18).

Not only were the Jews expecting the birth of a Great King, a Wise Man and a Savior, but Plato and Socrates also spoke of the Logos and of the Universal Wise Man "yet to come." Confucius spoke of "the Saint;" the Sibyls, of a "Universal King;" the Greek dramatist, of a savior and redeemer to unloose man from the "primal eldest curse." All these were on the Gentile side of the expectation. What separates Christ from all men is that first He was expected; even the Gentiles had a longing for a deliverer, or redeemer. This fact alone distinguishes Him from all other religious leaders. Jesus even acknowledged His pre-announcement when following His resurrection "beginning at Moses and all the prophets, he expounded" to the two men on the Emmaus road from "all the Scriptures the things concerning himself" (Luke 24:27).

A second distinguishing fact is that once He appeared, He struck history with such impact that He split it in two, dividing it into two periods: one before His coming, the other after it. Buddha did not do this, nor did any of the great Indian philosophers. Even those who deny God must date their attacks upon Him, BC, so and so, or AD so many years after His coming.

A third fact separating Him from all the others is this: every other person who ever came into this world came into it to live. He came into it to die. Death was a stumbling block to Socrates—it interrupted his teaching; but to Christ, death was the goal and fulfillment of His life, the goal that He was seeking. Few of His words or actions are intelligible without reference to His Cross. He presented Himself as a Savior rather than merely as a Teacher. It meant nothing to teach men to be good unless He also gave them the power to be good, after rescuing them from the frustration of guilt.

The story of every other human life begins with birth and ends with death. In the Person of Christ, however, it was His death that was first and His life that was last. The Scripture describes Him as "the Lamb slain as it were, from the beginning of the world" (I Peter 1:20). He was slain in intention by the first sin and rebellion against God. It was not so much that His birth cast a shadow on His life and thus led to His death; it was rather that the Cross was first, and cast its shadow back to His birth. His has been the only life in the world that was ever lived backward. As the flower in the crannied wall tells the poet of nature, and as the atom is the miniature of the solar system, so too, His birth tells the mystery of the gibbet. He went from the known to the known, from the reason of His coming manifested by His name "Jesus" or "Savior" to the fulfillment of His coming, namely, His death on the Cross.

A fourth distinguishing fact is that, unlike all other teachers who have come and gone, Christ left behind an empty tomb. The tomb of Mohammed is not an empty tomb; parts of Buddha's body are scattered all over the Orient; but Christ went into the tomb not to be held captive by it (Ps. 16:10), but to destroy its power. The resurrection had reversed the verdict of the Cross. The Messiah who had died there in weakness and in shame was not publicly acknowledged and proclaimed as the Messiah "with power." His resurrection is the guarantee that all those who die "in Him" shall live again (1. Cor. 15:16–22). Where in all other religions can you find a hope like that?

Apollo and the Other "Gods" or Jesus?

A fifth distinguishing fact is that He does not fit, as other world teachers do, into the established category of a good man. Good men do not lie; but if Christ was not all that He said He was, namely, the Son of the living God, the Word of God in the flesh, then He was not "just a good man;" then He was a knave, a liar, a charlatan and the greatest deceiver who ever lived. If He was only a man, then He was not even a "good" man.

However, He was not only a man. He would have us either despise Him or worship Him—despise Him as a mere man, or worship Him as true God and true man. That is the alternative He presents. If He is what He claimed to be, a Savior, a Redeemer, then we have a virile Christ and a leader worth following in these terrible times; One who will step into the breach of death, crushing sin, gloom and despair. We need a Christ today who will make cords and drive the buyers and sellers from our new temples, who will blast the unfruitful fig tree, who will talk crosses and sacrifices, and whose voice will be like the raging sea; but He will not allow us to pick and choose among His words, discarding the hard ones, and accepting the ones that please our fancy.

A decision about Christ cannot be avoided. With so many sane people all around us firmly believing that He is the Savior, we have to have an opinion about whether they are right or wrong. Your decision about Christianity is not a matter of spiritual speculation, but a conclusion about history. Bethlehem is not a fabled spot, like Camelot; it has a sports car dealership. Today in Jerusalem, city bus number 43 travels the route of Jesus' triumphal entry, leaving Bethany on the half-hour. Jesus is not a mythical figure, like Beowulf; there are few secular early first century references to Him, but no one doubts that someone of that name gave history a powerful twist, nearly twenty centuries ago. A dispute over the site of the temple He frequented affects what I pay for gasoline. If I begin to think of the Jews as characters in religious folklore, I need only walk down the street and look at the synagogue. What happened? Did Jesus actually come to the earth to open up the blessed life that a loving God intends for you? The answer to that can scarcely be, "I neither know nor care."

IV

GODS OF GOLD AND GRAVES OF ASHES

"I, a stranger and afraid
In a world I never made."

Many a man gazing in the "infinite meadows of heaven" where "blossomed the lovely stars" has felt like the poet and longed for assurance from One greater than himself. What would we not give for a single page from heaven which (1) proved the existence of a divine Father who ruled and overruled, (2) demonstrated that the Bible was the revealed word of this Ruler of the universe, (3) explained the past and foretold the future, (4) unfolded the Creator's secrets regarding how His creatures should live in order to have unalloyed joy forever?

Men have long sought such a page. In the non-Christian writings of philosophy and heathenism we have records of men searching for a revelation of truth. Sir Alfred Lyall expressed the dreary loneliness of that lack in his *Meditations of a Hindu Prince*:

"And the myriad idols around me, and the legion
  of muttering priests,
The revels and rites unholy, the dark unspeakable
  feasts!
What have they wrung from the Silence? Hath
  even a whisper come
Of the secret, Whence and Whither?
Alas! for the gods are dumb."

The longed-for oracle can be found only amid the prophetic writings of the Christian Guidebook. It is found exactly where Christ bade the people in our time to look. To those living just before His second return, He gave the admonition to understand Daniel the prophet (Matt. 24:15). Those who obey Him will not be disappointed. One page alone from this recommended source can answer the fundamental longings of the human heart.

An Adventure into Discovery

Unfortunately, too many people look upon Bible prophecy as the gospel minister's crystal ball, from which he discerns the image of coming events concerning the nations. But Bible prophecy is meant to be a mirror for every Christian, a mirror revealing his own destiny. It is not merely prediction, but comfort and guidance. It unfolds not only the secrets of time but the mysteries of eternity. Divine prophecy demonstrates that our world is a ship under control, rather than a wandering iceberg, and that our individual lives may be likewise. We are not alone–a scurrying, harassed leaf in a senseless universe.

Dr. A. T. Pierson affirms this line of thought when he says:

> "Prophecy and Providence are, therefore, twin sisters. There is no greater thought in this Bible than that, back of all these capricious, conflicting and accidental changes of human history, there is an infinite God, whose omniscience and omnipresence forbid that anything would escape his knowledge or evade his power, and whose goodness assures a benevolent design!
>
> *'Right forever on the scaffold, wrong forever on the throne!*
> *Yet that scaffold sways the future, and behind the great unknown,*
> *Standeth God amid the shadows, keeping watch above his own.'*
>
> "Prophecy, unmistakably outlining events before hand, shows that God is behind the curtain, and that His hand controls and shapes the history and destiny of men. The caprice is resolved into a consistent purpose; the conflict is only the apparent discord and disorder which are owing to our partial point of view; the accident becomes an incident in one grand, harmonious plan, where no chance can occur. We have a Providence, with its prevision and provision and presidence, directing and arranging, permitting and decreeing."[7]

I propose, therefore, that prophecy tells of a Providence which provides for all things and for every person.

Little wonder, then, that some of the greatest of human minds in recent centuries, heeding Christ's admonition, have found joy and profit in the prophetic pages of the Bible. Conspicuous among them was Sir Isaac Newton, certainly one of the outstanding scientists of all time. Few are aware that he probably spent more time on the prophecies of the Book of Daniel (which, along with the Book of Revelation, is the greatest book of prophecy in the entire bible) than on his study of gravitation.

This Old Testament book recommended by Christ for Christians living in our day contains prophecies extending to the "time of the end." (Dan. 12:3, 4). It presents a detailed chain of descriptions of the rise and fall of earth's most influential empires, from the days of Nebuchadnezzar (sixth century B.C.) till the ultimate establishment of the kingdom of God. Four times in Daniel's twelve-chapter book, the prophet previewed the centuries of the future in his day, and on each successive occasion beholding additional details filling out the original sketch. This original sketch (Daniel 2:31-45) contains a bird's-eye view of the events of three millennia and more. In just fifteen verses, the rise and fall of empires is set forth.

What a contrast this abbreviated historical survey to the story of Prince Zemire, who, upon succeeding his father on Persia's throne, sought for a guiding history of the past. Twenty years after the initial assembly of his learned men, a caravan of 12 camels, each bearing 500 volumes, came to the prince. After a speech, the secretary presented the 6,000 volumes. Now fully occupied with the duties of government, the king expressed his gratitude; but he added,

> "I am now middle-aged, and even if I live to be old, I shall not have time to read such a long history. Abridge it!"

Another score of years passed, and three camels with 1,500 volumes for the king. But he declared, "I am now an old man. Abridge further, and with all possible speed!"

After a lapse of ten years, a small elephant carried their abbreviated work, this time merely 500 volumes. "We have been exceedingly brief," said the remaining members of the assembly.

"Not yet sufficiently so," replied the king. "My life is almost over. Abridge again!"

When, after five more years, the secretary returned alone, and on crutches, leading a small donkey burdened with one large book, the king was breathing his last, unable to read it.

Yet in 213 words the prophet Daniel described the course of history and its meaning more accurately than all the historians of the ages!

However, before we examine this Old Testament prophecy, let us visit the place where Daniel received this remarkable vision. Our journey takes us to Bagdad, the capital city of the revolution-torn country of Iraq. Just 65 miles south of this city of Arabian Night fame by the river Euphrates sprawls a pile of rubble around several large dirt mounds.

A notice by the side of the road indicates that this is all that remains of one of the largest cities of ancient times, but is now just graves of ashes. As the eye surveys this ruin, the line of Thomas A'Kempis comes to mind, "O how quickly passes away the glory of the earth."

It was certainly true of Babylon, because once this city was the mistress of the world, second only to Thebes of Egypt. She worked out problems in arithmetic; invented implements for measuring time; conceived the plan of building enormous structures with the poorest of building materials–clay; discovered the art of polishing, boring and engraving gems; knew how to faithfully reproduce the outlines of human and animal remains; attained a high perfection in textile fabrics; studied successfully the movements of the stars; conceived of grammar as a science; elaborated a system of law; and saw the value of exact chronology. In almost every branch of science this great city made a beginning. In fact, much of the learning of Greece and Rome had its origin in Babylon.

This was a city whose towering walls and lofty palace structures were legend and whose hanging gardens were one of the wonders of the ancient world. According to the German archaeologist, Robert Koldeway–who excavated Babylon before the First World War–the gardens were built in a series of wide, sweeping terraces, rising like a flight of stairs to a height of nearly four hundred feet. These terraces, supported by heavy arches, held thick layers of soil, sufficient to maintain the growth, not only of grass and flowers, but quite large fruit-bearing trees. The gardens were irrigated by hydraulic pumps, which would have to be worked by hand or perhaps by oxen–we do not know. The platforms would be ablaze with the color of flowers from the remotest parts of Asia, and shaded from the too-hot sun by trees, laden in season with fruits. The air would be heavy with the scent of flowers, wafted through screens of cooling water into the sumptuous inner chambers where the royal family held their splendid court. Today, two millennia later, while archaeologists verify the facts of Babylon's magnificence, the city is in ruins just graves of ashes.

However, beneath the dust of antiquity can still be seen traces of that magnificence about which King Nebuchadnezzar could boast when he said, "Is not this great Babylon which I have built?" (Daniel 4:30). When Koldeway excavated here, he found an inscription by Nebuchadnezzar that verified this exclamation of the king. It read (translated from a cuneiform inscription):

> "Then I built the palace, the seat of my royalty, the bond of the race of men, the dwelling of exultation and rejoicing."

As I sat in those dusty, miserable ruins reflecting upon the fate of this once great metropolis, I was again reminded of the warnings that two of the Hebrew prophets directed towards this mighty city. A century and a

An Adventure into Discovery

half before Babylon fell, Isaiah prophesied with startling specificity:

> "And Babylon, the glory of the kingdoms...shall be as when God overthrew Sodom and Gomorrah. It shall never be inhabited, neither shall it be dwelt in...neither shall the Arabian pitch tent there; neither shall the shepherds make their fold there. But wild beasts of the desert shall lie there; and their houses shall be full of doleful creatures; and owls shall dwell there..."–Isaiah 13:19-22.

Later, Jeremiah with equal vehemence thundered his warning:

> "And Babylon shall become heaps, a dwelling place for dragons, an astonishment, and an hissing, without an inhabitant."–Jeremiah 5 1:37

How true the forecast, because Babylon has been uninhabited since the third century B.C., apart from those who came to the site in order to quarry her bricks! Alexander the Great had visions of restoring the city to its original splendor and making it his new world capital. He died and the work was suspended. By the Christian era, Babylon had been so reduced that the Persian kings were using what remained of the walls as enclosures for wild animals. The city was sunk into oblivion, a confusion of mud-brick mounds. The frescoed walls of state, bright with candelabra, the gold-inlaid furniture, the wine goblets, the slaves and dancing

Reconstruction of the Ishtar Gate

Golds of God and Graves of Ashes

girls, the flower-fined, tree-shaded terraces and the water which fed them, all are gone. All that remains are broken walls, cellars and empty wells where slaves and animals toiled endlessly in the darkness...

Squatting in the shade of a palm tree with sweat dripping onto the page of my open Bible, I pondered the remarkable prophecy and asked the questions that have been voiced for centuries: How did the prophet know that Babylon would be uninhabited? Other lesser cities like Jerusalem, Rome, and Constantinople have survived the ages as cities of consequence since their foundation! Why has Babylon become "graves of ashes?" How did the prophet know that the Arab would not pitch his tent there? How did the prophet know that this place would become perpetually desolate, "heaps," and her walls broken down? Furthermore, how did the prophet know that the Babylonians as a people would die out but that the Arab would continue to live on? Frankly, in all my travels, I have yet to meet a person who will say to me, "I am a Babylonian!"

I turned the soiled pages of my Bible and read the answer:

> "...I am God, and there is none else; I am God and there is none like me, declaring the end from the beginning, and from ancient times the things that are not yet done..."–Isaiah 49:9, 10.

The author of these prophecies was a God before whom the future was an open book. And the ruins of Babylon, with their once lavishly-adorned images and broken walls, are another evidence that there is in existence a God who can with certainty declare the things of the future.

So the prophet answers our fundamental human need as it gives the assurance, "There is a God in heaven that revealeth secrets" (Daniel 2:28). We live in an age which has endeavored to outlaw God and revelation by stress on the absolute reign of physical law. The materialistic

An Adventure into Discovery

science of the past three centuries and the philosophy of men such as Kant have asserted that the laws of nature operate uniformly, inexorably, and independently of any divine Lawgiver. Thus the universe is represented as a closed system, unable to reveal to its prisoner any sure knowledge of the supernal realms beyond.

Both scientists and philosophers have forgotten that, although a bird may not fly out of its atmosphere, the Creator of the bird and atmosphere is free to insert his finger into time and space and place it lovingly upon the bird. There is a God in heaven that revealeth secrets, and He has intervened in history to offer man revelation and redemption.

Away back in the sixth century B.C., when Babylon ruled the world, Daniel recorded a dream that unfolded not only world history subsequent to his times, but also the political future of our times. The reigning monarch of the day, Nebuchadnezzar, contemplating the political future of his own times, dreamed of a huge image with golden head, silver chest, brass belly and thighs, iron legs and feet partly of iron and partly of clay (Daniel 2:30-36). Daniel told the king that in these symbols was a preview

Cuneiform Inscription of Nebuchanezzar

of future events that stretched to modern times (Daniel 2:28, 29). Daniel gave the following detailed explanation of the metal man:

> "Thou art this head of gold. And after thee shall arise another kingdom inferior to thee, and another third kingdom of brass, which shall bear rule over all the earth. And the fourth kingdom shall be strong as iron: forasmuch as iron breaketh in pieces and subdueth all things: and as iron that breaketh all these, shall it break in pieces and bruise. And whereas thou sawest the feet and toes, part of potters' clay, and part of iron, the kingdom shall be divided; but there shall be in it of the strength of the iron, forasmuch as thou sawest iron mixed with miry clay. And as the toes of the feet were part of iron, and part of clay, so the kingdom shall be partly strong, and partly broken. And whereas thou sawest iron mixed with miry clay, they shall mingle themselves with the seed of men: but they shall not cleave one to another, even as iron is not mixed with clay. And in the days of these kings shall the God of heaven set up a kingdom, which shall never be destroyed: and the kingdom shall not be left to other people, but it shall break in pieces and consume all these kingdoms, and it shall stand forever."–*Daniel* 2:38-44.

To read the record foretelling the future course of the centuries brings inevitable conviction to the honest heart. It is an undeniable fact that from Daniel's time to our own four great empires have succeeded each other, increasing in size and in significance for the church and the world. These four are Babylon, Medo-Persia, Greece, and Rome. Consult any ancient history that covers the days from the seventh century B.C. to the present; or consider that the most famous of historical records, the Canon of Ptolemy, which sets out the ages under the headings of the kings of Babylon, Medo-Persia, Greece, and Rome. Why, even the first century B.C. Roman poet, Ovid, in his Metamorphosis, divides world history into the golden, silver, bronze and iron ages! Finally, review the pages of Holy Writ, and note that from the time of Israel's submission to the Neo-Babylonian Empire until the final pages of the New

Testament, only four mighty empires are named, those symbolized by the metallic sections of the image.[8]

Four civilization-molding powers, extending like concentric circles in strength and conquest until the whole of what we know as Europe would be absorbed, were foretold by this page from the Old Testament prophet Daniel. The fourth empire, Rome, was to be divided into fragments of varying strength, which in futile fashion would throughout all later years endeavor to weld themselves into yet another empire. Ultimately, a fifth empire would indeed arise, but it would be one divine in origin and rulership. The prophetic statement regarding the nations which sprang from old Rome–*"they shall not cleave one to another"*–has been confirmed by over fifteen centuries of bloody but fruitless war, and by the barren intrigues of statecraft over that same period.

Consider the following comment from *The New York Times* library supplement of December 28, 1946:

> "How has the continent of Europe escaped political unification? Everything in Europe seems to call for it; everything, that is, except the temperament and traditions of its people. More uniform in climate than China, less diverse in religion than India, less diverse in race than the United States of America, Europe has had for centuries a single culture and a common social structure. Landowner and peasant, merchant and banker, factory owner and factory worker, artist and scholar, would nowhere find themselves in an alien world in moving from one part of the continent to another... For a thousand years men have dreamed of European union; yet for a thousand years this most uniform of continents has defied political unification."

The truth of this editorial is reinforced as one recalls the architects of European unity: Charlemagne, Charles V, Louis XIV and Napoleon; in the modern era, Kaiser Wilhelm and Hitler. What tears and sweat and blood has been the portion of sorrowing humanity because men have failed to mark well what God has declared concerning the division of Western Europe.

The writer of the above editorial comments on the Hitler dream:

> "Never before had a plan for world conquest been worked out with such scientific precision, nor was one ever before carried out with such savage ruthlessness. In comparison, even the undertakings of Alexander, Napoleon, and Wilhelm II look almost impoverished and amateurish...And yet it failed. Why did it fail?"

The prophetic statement–*"they shall not cleave one to another"*–gives answer. Fifteen centuries of bloody and fruitless war, as well as the barren intrigues of statecraft over the same period, give confirmation.

Had Daniel written out of his own imagination, why should he have stopped at four in predicting coming empires in Asia and Europe? Why not fourteen? Or forty? Surely if Babylon was to give way to Medo-Persia, and Medo-Persia to Greece, and Greece to Rome, would not Rome likewise give way to another, and that conqueror to yet another, and so on? The fulfillment of this prophecy of Daniel 2 is alone sufficient to demonstrate the inspiration of the Bible and the fact that our world is not a runaway.

Almost two thousand years ago, the Jewish historian Josephus drew this lesson for the pagan Epicureans of his day, who believed in the reign of chance and flux. He reviewed the prophecies of Daniel regarding the four dominant empires of the past, and then added:

> "All these things did this man (Daniel) leave in writing, as God had showed them to him, insomuch that such as read his prophecies, and see how they have been fulfilled, would wonder at the honor wherewith God honored Daniel and may thence discover how the Epicureans are in error, who cast Providence out of human life, and do not believe that God takes care of the affairs of the world, nor that the universe is governed

47

and continued in being by that blessed and immortal nature, but say that the world is carried along by its own accord, without a ruler,...like ships without pilots, which we see drowned by the winds, or like chariots without drivers, which are overturned; so would the world be dashed to pieces by its being carried without Providence, and so perish and come to naught."[9]

Thus we have abundant evidence for the four points suggested in the introduction: (1) evidence for the existence of an omnipotent God who rules and overrules; (2) evidence demonstrating that the Bible is the reliable Word of this omnipotent God; (3) evidence that the past is explained (in Daniel 2) and the future foretold. And before we come to the fourth, a final firm note about the future. The prophecy of Daniel 2 makes it clear that human history will not terminate with the mushroom clouds of man's devising, but by the inter-position of God in human affairs. God's pledge is, that the fifth universal empire will be the "kingdom of our Lord and of His Christ; and He shall reign forever and ever." (Rev. 11:15) The next great event on the stage of human history is the Second Coming of Jesus to whom earth's crown belongs. "And in the days of these kings shall the God of heaven set up a kingdom, which shall never be destroyed." (Daniel 2:44).

Like a mighty beacon, this amazing prophecy shines down through the centuries, illuminating the great events of time–glittering on the gold of Babylon; shimmering on the silver of Medo-Persia; glinting on the brass of Greece, shining on the iron of Rome; lighting up the struggles and conflict of our modern world; and glows at last on the face of the King of Kings in returning glory. In the days of our broken, bleeding kingdoms, the King Himself will write "Finish" to man's attempts to govern himself.

Now what about the fourth point? Does this remarkable prophecy also explain how men should live in order to live forever?

The All-wise One does not reveal secrets that we may be merely intellectually informed. His predictions mirror eternal truths and indicate the principles which should govern all our words and deeds. Let us inquire: How did Christ interpret the chief import of this prophecy? In Matthew 21:44 we have His comment: "Whosoever shall fall on this stone shall be broken: but on whomsoever it shall fall, it will grind him to powder." Christ saw in Daniel 2 that only those who are one with God could withstand the cataclysm of the end of the age. Only those built on Himself, the Rock of Ages, would grow eternally with the kingdom of God. Only those who surrendered their self-will until it was completely broken could avoid being ground to dust.

It is thus evident that to Christ prophecy was not merely a road map of events. It was loving counsel from the Creator to the creature, revealing what most needed to be known regarding duty. Christ saw that only a right understanding concerning eternity could enable man to live rightly in time, and similarly, that a true concept of time sheds light on man's preparation for eternity.

The prophecy of Daniel 2 makes it plain that all things earthly, however grand, must deteriorate unless linked with God. Consider the gradual deterioration shown by the symbolism of the metal man. With the passing of the years there is transition from gold to silver, from silver to brass, from brass to iron and clay, and finally to nothingness after the very dust has been blown away as the chaff from a threshing floor. The picture is clear: from gods of gold to graves of ashes is the testimony of time.

There is deterioration also suggested by the increasing multiplicity in the symbolism of the image. From the single symbol of the head of gold we pass to the dual symbol of breast and arms, and then to the presentation of stomach and thighs. This is succeeded by the decimal picture of the toes, and then ultimately the myriad scattered specks of dust. In value and in specific gravity the parts of the image reflect the same lesson of deterioration. While proud man since the eighteenth-century enlightenment has rejoiced in the law of progress, twentieth-century events have endorsed the principle expressed in this prophecy that apart from God all things human deteriorate rather than improve. And what is true of the conglomerate is also true of the individual. You and I are on our way to decay and eternal nothingness unless we take hold of divine power. "How shall we escape, if we neglect so great salvation?" (Hebrews 2:3).

Why did Babylon go down in drunken dishonor during the impious feast of Belshazzar when he was toasting to gods of gold? Why did Medo-Persia, Greece, and Rome each fail to endure? What was their fatal weakness or mistake? The answer is that to each came the gospel through God's messengers, but each rejected it. Proud Babylon ignored the warnings of Daniel, and the cruel Medo-Persians condemned to death the whole race of Esther the Jewess. World-wise Greeks refused to be instructed by the books of the feeble Jews, and the Romans slew not only the Son of God but multitudes of His disciples. In thunderous tones history is proclaiming the solemn warning of Scripture:

> "That the world passeth away, and the lust thereof;
> but he that doeth the will of God abideth for ever."
> (I John 2:17).

Such is the divine admonition in the prophecy recommended by our Lord for study. But on the same page is to be found heavenly comfort. The growth of the tiny pebble into a mountain filling the earth for eternity is parabolic of the fact that believers in Christ, though despised like Him, will continually increase and prosper regardless of all transitory events. Those who now permit their sinful habits to be broken by Christ's gospel, those who receive *"forgiveness of sins,"* need not henceforth be anxious *"about anything."* (Philippians 4:6, R.S.V.) To be wholly dependent upon God is to become independent of all else. This prophecy assures the believer that God's love overrules all chance and change.

It is not true that *"history teaches us that history teaches us nothing."* History is indeed His-story. Christ is no absentee Landlord, permitting His house to disintegrate through careless tenants. The right reading of history brings the assurance that what God made He governs, and the He who controls the cosmos also guides the atom.

The God who saved Europe repeatedly from the Mohammedan Turks and England from the galleons of Spain; the God who provided the new continent of America for those denied religious freedom in the Old World; the God who toppled the mighty empires of Babylon, Medo-Persia, Greece and Rome–that God guides all His children, making *"all things work together for good"* to even the least believer.

> *"The night brings forth the morn–*
> *Of the cloud is the lightning born,*
> *From out the darkest earth the brightest roses grow.*
> *Bright sparks from black flints fly,*
> *And from out a leaden sky*
> *Comes the silvery-footed spirit of the snow."*
>   —Denis Florence MacCarthy

V
SECRETS IN STONE

"That God, which ever lives and loves,
One God, one law, one element,
And one far-off divine event,
To which the whole creation moves."
—Tennyson

"What a waste it would be after four billion torturous years of evolution if the dominant organism contrived its own self-destruction," Carl Sagan, popular guardian of the cosmos and professor of astronomy at Cornell, told a crowd of 2,000 in Ithaca, New York. "We are the first species to have devised the means." George Kistiakowsky, an advisor to President Dwight Eisenhower who had worked on the Manhattan Project, told a Harvard audience: "If I knew then what I know now, I never would have helped to develop the bomb." For centuries people have feared the war to end all wars, the ultimate holocaust, the unthinkable catastrophe, the final destruction when the whole world is dragged over the precipice and into the bottomless pit.

Whole-hearted endorsement for nuclear pacifism was vehemently expressed by Roman Catholic bishops at Vatican II: "Any act of war aimed indiscriminately at the destruction of entire cities or of extensive areas along with their population is a crime against God and man himself. It merits unequivocal and unhesitating condemnation".[10] We shrink from the thought of it, but the possibility has a macabre fascination.

There is a suicidal streak in us all, says Alvarez in his book The Savage God. He suggests *"The Savage God"* lures us to the very brink, and then we draw back only to return to the scene of temptation again and again—and of course each time we get closer to the edge. We try to pretend if anything did happen it would be accidental. Every attempt is made to cover up the suicidal nature of our activities; like the Irish coroner who said of a man who blew his head off: "Sure, he was only trying to clean the muzzle of his gun with his tongue!"

The urge to self-destruction is difficult to explain. Arthur Koestler speaks of something going wrong during the last explosive stages of evolution. There seems to be a flaw, a subtle engineering mistake built into our native equipment. Perhaps the circuiting of our nervous system makes us prone to delusions and goads us toward self-destruction. We are an aberrant species "suffering from a biological malfunction, a specific disorder of behavior which sets us apart from all other animal species".[11]

Our neo-cortex has developed at such a rapid and explosive speed that we are permanently handicapped. Newly-developing structures have not become properly integrated with older ones. Our emotional and intellectual behaviors clash and, as a result, we are constantly at war with ourselves and with others. Since we unlocked the forces in the atomic nucleus we have had to live with the distinct possibility of our death as a species. We carry a time-bomb fastened around our necks. We shall have to listen to the sound of its ticking now softer, now louder again for decades and centuries to come, until it either blows up or we succeed in defusing it. However, if Vietnam, Ireland, Bangladesh, the Falkland Islands, New York, and the Middle East are any guide, we're not very successful at defusing bombs.

The failure of the United Nations to settle any sizeable dispute thus far is proof that old emotions get the better part of the argument, and that we are really punch-drunk and very dangerous. We reckon we don't like violence, but one evening's television viewing or one excursion to the cinema and theater settles that. We love violence. Ian Fleming was quick enough to recognize how potent and profitable a mixture of sex and sadism can be. Now everyone is following suit, and the danger that our obsession will turn inwards and destroy us is very real. In a world where there are so many suicides, so many more attempted suicides, so much deliberately willed self-destruction (alcohol, nicotine, drugs, road accidents, etc.), the chance of global suicide is a distinct possibility.

"We are faced," wrote Bertrand Russell, "with a very grim question, namely, can scientific man survive, or is the mixture of advanced knowledge with primitive undisciplined passion so unchangeable as to make human survival improbable?...If we may judge by the actions of great states, and by the public opinion which supports these actions, it is a characteristic of *Homo Sapiens* that he is more anxious to kill his enemies than to stay alive himself".[12]

The end is too close to be comfortable. During the days of the Enlightenment, when the future was rosy and heaven was just around the corner, people believed that war was outmoded. Sweet reason assured them that all good things come to those who put their trust in man. "His moral capacity to grow in virtue, his rational capacity to read the laws of nature and thus to harness nature to his use; his ability also to engineer society as well as physical nature, and ultimately to reduce life to a rational plan; in a word, to accomplish in time what had previously been considered to be the work of eternity, to carve out on earth a great kingdom or empire of man, morally, better and intellectually superior to anything that had gone before"[13] guaranteed lasting peace.

Splendid though the vision was, it never materialized and all the time we were steadily but inexorably approaching the point of disaster.

Now the words of Jesus seem much more fitting than the platitudes of false prophets who prophesied peace when there was none. "And there shall be signs in sun and moon and stars, and upon the earth dismay among nations, in perplexity at the roaring of the sea and the waves, men fainting from fear and the expectations of the things, which are coming upon the world; for the powers of the heavens will be shaken. And then they will see the Son of man coming in a cloud with power and great glory" (Luke 21:25-27, *NASB*).

The setting is up-to-date; it fits the human situation. That is the gripping thing about the Bible. The book is ageless. The timeliness and the timelessness of Scripture is unique. Its colors never fade; they go on and on, and on, illuminating centuries, casting light on crises upon crises in a telescopic fashion. Today they are just as vivid as when they were spoken two-thousand years ago. "The message of the prophets," said Peter, "is like a lamp shining in a murky place, until the daybreaks and the morning star rises to illuminate your minds" (*2 Peter* 1:19).

Some years ago, the eminent philosopher-theologian J. V. Langmead Casserly discussed the biblical theme of the end of the world in a series of BBC broadcasts. He made the observation that "we seem to be reaching a stage in history at which it is possible for the sin and folly of man to bring about the end of the world, the kind of conclusion to human history to which many of the biblical passages seem to point. As we read these passages... we can hardly refrain from saying to ourselves, 'Yes, it could be very like that, indeed, it could be just that.'"

He continued, "Even before the coming of nuclear fission there were good scientific grounds for believing that one day the world would have to end, that human life could not continue indefinitely on this planet."

Certainly the writers of the Bible held no delusions about that; and further, they knew that end time events would focus on their world, the Middle East. There is a deep feeling that since human history began in the region between the five seas—the Black Sea, the Caspian, the Mediterranean, the Red Sea, and the Persian Gulf—it might also end there. To the Christian as well as the Jew, human existence is seen against the backdrop of the Middle East. Adam and Eve lived in a garden somewhere in the vicinity of the Persian Gulf. Abraham migrated from Chaldea to southern Palestine. The Patriarchs pastured flocks on the West Bank of the Jordan. After a period of exile in Egypt, the nation of Israel was forged by Moses in the wilderness of Sinai. Canaan was settled. Zion was established. The temple of God was erected by Solomon. Although the tribes were dispersed into Assyria and Babylonia, a remnant returned and rebuilt Jerusalem to last forever. Somehow it was felt that if the capital fell once more the world would end. In fact, when Jesus spoke to His disciples of the destruction of Jerusalem and its temple, they associated the catastrophe with the end of the world (Matthew 24:1-3).

The Old City of Jerusalem from the Church of Dominus Flevit

The temple standing in Jerusalem in the days of Jesus was built in the second decade B.C. by Herod the Great. That temple, just like the Jerusalem of the Gospels, is gone. The latter lies far below the level of the present city. Actually, the walls of the existing "old city" were built by the Turks under their great ruler Sultan Suleiman the Magnificent (1450). These walls, which are about two and a half miles in circumference, have 34 towers and eight gates. On entering the Jaffa Gate, to the right is a big tower, the "tower of David." The huge blocks of masonry at the base of this tower date back to the time of Herod the Great. The reason why they were left standing when the rest of the city was destroyed was because the Citadel was used as a garrison for Roman soldiers when Jerusalem was sacked in A.D. 70.

Dominating the skyline of walled Jerusalem is the famous *Dome of the Rock*, sometimes erroneously called the *Mosque of Omar*. The Dome was built in the seventh century of the Christian era by Abdul Malek, and is the earliest example of Arabic architecture still in existence.

Secrets in Stone

Built on an elevated platform, it is approached by flights of steps surmounted by arches. The mosque is octagonal in shape, and above it on a cylindrical drum the dome rises to a height of 108 feet. The exterior is covered with grey-veined white marble, and the upper part with fine porcelain tiles. The dome, made of plates of aluminum impregnated with gold, gleams in the brilliant sunshine.

Harem es Sharif, as it is called by the Arabs, is built on a huge stone platform that formed the base of the magnificent Temple of Herod. While the Moslem sanctuary is certainly a beautiful building, it is nothing compared with the splendid structure that stood there in Christ's day. We know what it was like from the descriptions of Josephus, the Mishnah, as well as from the archaeological evidence from the present site. An actual reconstruction of this temple can be seen today in that part of Jerusalem called "New Jerusalem."

The Wailing Wall

Nothing is left of that temple today except a pile of stone rubble and one small part of the outer enclosure called the "Wailing Wall." Here, Jews assemble to wail over the destruction of their temple and pray for its reconstruction. If stones had ears, what lamentations and the miseries and atrocities and lost glories could be heard! I was amazed to discover the size of the stones that comprise this part of the wall. They average nine to fifteen feet in length and three to four feet in height. The largest is a whopping 36 feet in length and weighs nearly 100 tons. No wonder the massive walls and splendid building of the Temple evoked general admiration amongst the Jews and Gentiles. They made a great impression on the disciples of Jesus too. Of course, like the Jews, they thought this wonderful temple would last forever, but Jesus saw further than they when He forecast "not one stone here shall be left upon another, which will not be torn down" (Matthew 24:2).

Peter, James and John were amazed at His strange words. Later they asked Him privately, as He sat on the Mount of Olives, when His fateful words would come true, what signs would precede the disaster, and whether such an event would mark the end of the world (verse 3). Jesus proceeded to answer the first of their questions by describing in detail the overthrow of Jerusalem (an even then 39 years in the future). He told them of "false Messiahs" who would try to deliver the Jews from the cursed Romans (verse 5). He spoke of rumors of wars (verse 6). Terrible trouble would befall the nation (verse 22). Famines, pestilence and earthquakes (verse 7). Unbelievable persecution (verse 9), and finally the rape of their glorious temple (verse 15).

It was not long until those three men saw their Master's words come true. In A.D. 70, Titus marched his Roman legions against Jerusalem. Dead Sea cave finds have provided evidence of guerrilla tactics employed against the Romans at this time. Josephus, a first century Jewish historian, in his *Wars* describes the terrible panic, the harrowing hunger, the disease ridden city, the looting, torture, mass crucifixions. It was a bloody business and hovering over it all were supernatural portents announcing the doom of the Temple. Tacitus, the classical historian, recorded that at the height of the siege the 75-foot high golden doors of the holy place mysteriously swung open and a superhuman voice cried "the gods are departing".[14] Finally the temple was burned to the ground.

Jesus had accurately forecast the destruction of the temple and the sacking of Jerusalem; but there was more to this apocalyptic discussion given on the gentle slopes of Olivet. Following the fall of the Jewish nation, Jesus forecast that the Christian church would pass through a period of "tribulation" (*Matthew* 24:11). Judaism would find its extension in Christianity. Caesar, not knowing the difference, set about to liquidate this new "sect of the Jews." So it was, for the next three centuries after A.D. 70, ten awful persecutions rolled up against the frail bark of the Christian church, as thousands of faithful sealed their testimony with their own blood. From Nero in A.D. 67 to Constantine's *Edict of Toleration* in A.D. 303, the church "*sailed through bloody seas.*"

Two centuries of brief respite followed the "Era of the Martyrs" and then the Dark Ages, when, according to "credible historians ...more than fifty million of the human family (were) slaughtered for the crime of heresy...".[15]

However, there was more to Jesus' prophecy. He said that these days of trial would be followed by several unusual natural phenomena. The sun would be darkened, the moon would not shine, and the stars would appear to fall out of the sky (Matthew 24:29).

History has been called the "unrolled scroll of prophecy," and once again the words of Jesus were fulfilled by historical events. An ecclesiastical tyranny which had bound the souls of men for more than a thousand years was broken by a new individualism, Napoleonic expansionism, and the opening up of the "New World" for the religiously oppressed. This new day was greeted by an astronomical event when, at eleven o'clock on the morning of May 19, 1780, according to Webster's Dictionary under the subtitle "Dark Day," it began to grow dark as if night were coming. "Birds sang their evening song, disappeared, and became silent; fowls went to their roosts; candles were lighted in the houses." The Connecticut State Legislature in session on that day was stunned into silence by the uncanny darkness. One member rallied sufficiently to move that the assembly adjourn. Abraham Davenport opposed the motion by saying:

> "I am against adjournment. The day of judgment is either approaching or it is not. If it is not, there is no cause for an adjournment; if it is, I choose to be found doing my duty. I wish therefore that candles be brought".[16]

Webster admitted that "the true cause of this phenomenon is not known." He was right. The event could not find its explanation by an eclipse, for no eclipse produces total darkness and the position of the sun in relation to the earth made it impossible.

The already shaken nerves of those who had witnessed the Dark Day were upset the following night when the moon came into view. Its usual pure reflected light was replaced by a dull, angry shade of red. It appeared as an omen of impending doom. One wild-eyed observer made the comment:

> "I could not help conceiving at the time, that if every luminous body in the universe had been shrouded in impenetrable shades or struck out of existence, the darkness could not have been more complete...After midnight the darkness disappeared, and the moon, when first visible, had the appearance of blood."[17]

Jesus forecast a third astronomical event, "the stars shall fall from heaven." Did they? Reporting on such a phenomenon, C. G. Dolmade wrote: "Surpassing all displays of this kind ever seen, was that of November 13, 1833, when meteors fell thick as snowflakes." This remarkable event, seen from Canada to Mexico, continued for five hours, and some observatories estimated that the "stars" were falling at the rate of 200,000 per hour.

Astronomy witnesses to the truth of these three prophecies. These three sky signs marched across the heavens in the correct order and at the exact time forecast by Jesus. Was the hand of God reaching down into our solar system, veiling the face of the sun, interfering with the moon's color, and creating a celestial fireworks display in order to set the stage for end-time events? It seems likely, for Jesus prophesied that following these three sky signs, international distress would sweep the world and men would be overcome with a sense of failure. Human problems would escape resolution and the hearts of men would be filled with fear (Luke 21:25-27).

Twenty-first century events make it clear we are there! "If society continues its present course, we will unquestionably enter another dark age." So concluded the late Robert Lindner, well-known psychiatrist and a consultant to Maryland's state prison system, in an article in *The New York Times*. Dorothy Thompson thought we had already entered it when she wrote, "We are in a new Dark Ages. We are in it up to the neck!" An editorial entitled "Will History Repeat?" appeared in an issue of the Pacific Gas and Electric Company's magazine *Progress*. It listed five conditions which prevailed in the Roman Empire before its collapse:

"The undermining of the dignity and sanctity of the home, which is the basis for human society.

"Higher and higher taxes; the spending of public money for free bread and circuses for the populace.

"The mad craze for pleasure; sports becoming every year more exciting, more brutal, more immoral.

"The building of great armaments when the real enemy was within—the decay of individual responsibility.

"The decay of religion; faith fading into mere form, losing touch with life, losing power to guide the people.

"The oft-heard warning that 'history repeats itself,'" said the editor, "has an ominous meaning in the light of the above."

Then he added these even more challenging sentences: "The average age of the world's great civilizations has been 200 years." Is the cycle inevitable? There are many who write that unless drastic changes are made immediately—"yes!"

The late Charles P. Snow, British author and statesman, offers a solution that would bring about changes for the better. First, there must be a concerted effort by the rich countries to assist the poor. Second, the poor countries must strive to revolutionize their food production. Third, there must be a world reduction in population increase. To accomplish these objectives will require vast expenditures: "perhaps 20% of the gross national product of the rich countries for 10-15 years with major curbs in military spending." Then he asked:

> "Does anybody believe this will happen? We are all selfish. Political memory lasts about a week and political foresight stretches about another week ahead. To stint ourselves to avoid a disaster in 20 years—what body of people would ever do it?"[18]

An editorial that appeared over five decades ago resonates with the pessimism of the present:

> "As the bid for inhabitable space and arable land increases, the probability of nuclear war increases, with the ultimate forms of destruction destroying the highest forms of life. It is enough to make man believe that he is gripped by a demiurge which wants his death and which one or the other will bring his brief career to an end?"[19]

Why are these hard-hearted editors and political analysts so gloomy? Because the conditions prevailing in society today not only parallel closely the conditions which prevailed in Rome shortly before its fall, but the rate of decline has already surpassed that of Rome and continues to increase rapidly. The London *Fortnightly* announced ominously: "A survey of the world leaves one with the uncomfortable feeling that in spite of the efforts of many well-intentioned men in every country, civilization is sliding downhill."

One does not have to be a university professor to sense the meaning of all this. Christ's *"little apocalypse"* points unmistakably across the years to our day. The same Omniscient Eye that saw the siege of Jerusalem in the stones of Herod's Temple wall saw the fearful conditions of our time. Once we realize this, the sacred writings of the Bible are no longer old-fashioned ideas clothed in oriental language. They are vital to an understanding of contemporary affairs.

There was a time when scientists and philosophers tossed aside Bible statements about the world's end. They thought apocalyptic messages were naive in a world that science would make safe for centuries. The future was bright, they told us, man was on the threshold of better things, his prospects were limitless; but how wrong they have been—terribly wrong, for humanity seems to have come to a place where, in the words of H. G. Wells, there is "no way out" where all our leaders with their plans and proposals represent "little men with little minds throwing little words at gigantic problems." A modern writer compares our time to "an elephant hanging from a cliff with its tail tied to a daisy." Referring to the world's dilemma, a senior I. S. Government official states, "The handwriting on the wall of five continents now tells us that the day of judgment is at hand."[21]

Every Bible writer who had anything to say about this subject made it plain that this earth would one day come to a cataclysmic end, and in the forefront of these forecasters was the Master Prophet, Jesus. He said, "When you see these things happening, recognize that the Kingdom of God is near." (Luke 21:31). I see no reason to treat these words lightly. All He had to say about Jerusalem and A.D. 70 came true, and this will too, for He added, "My words will never pass away" (Luke 21:33).

Men talk of "peace, peace, when there is no peace" (Jeremiah 6:14), but man will not find the secret of lasting peace (1 Thessalonians 5:3). Will he destroy this lovely earth? He will come within a hair's breadth of doing so. Just as he is about to end human history, God steps in. "Then the sign of the Son of Man will appear in the sky, and then all the tribes of the earth will mourn, and they shall see the Son of Man coming on the clouds of the sky with power and great glory" (Matthew 24:30).

How will the end come? A scientific conference in Washington on "The World after Nuclear War" answers: "One billion people killed before the mushroom cloud even dissipates...an equal number doomed to slow, agonizing deaths. And then the nuclear war claims its next victim: planet Earth. Months of twilight shroud the globe and temperatures plunge 55 degrees, killing nearly all plant life. The ecological systems that once supported the earth become so devastated that 'the potential effects extend even to the extermination of *Homo sapiens*.'"[22]

The Bible answer is different and to the contrary. Jesus Christ, the Creator of the atom, will come and take control and "destroy them which destroy the earth" (Revelation 11:18). Only then will the vision of Pope Paul VI of *"war no more, war never again"* be realized. Only Christ's return can solve the ever-growing population explosion when He comes to set up His kingdom, from which will be excluded all vile and shameless people, "and sorcerers and fornicators and murderers and adulterers and everyone who loves and practices falsehood" (Revelation 22:15, RSV). The citizens of that kingdom "shall dwell in a peaceable habitation, and in sure dwellings, and in quiet resting places" (Isaiah 32:18). Christ's return is the answer to the problem of famine and the global water crisis. The citizens of His kingdom "shall hunger no more, neither thirst any more...For the Lamb which is in the midst of the throne shall feed them, and shall lead them unto living fountains of waters: and God will wipe away all tears from their eyes" (Revelation 7:16, 17).

Sadly, the second coming of Christ will be a time of judgment for some when they will quickly face the ultimate reality of their rebelliousness. As Jude writes, "I saw the Lord come with myriads of angels, to bring all men to judgment and to convict all the godless of all the godless deeds they have committed, and of all the defiant words which godless sinners had spoken against him" (Jude 15).

It needs emphasizing that, for those who have accepted Jesus and the provisions of salvation, the second coming is an event to be joyfully anticipated. It will be a time of resurrection, translation and eternal reunion, for "the dead in Christ shall rise first; and we which are alive and remain shall be caught up together with them in the clouds and so we shall ever be with the Lord" (1 Thessalonians 4:16, 17). A time of retribution, yes, but also an occasion for deliverance. "At that time thy people shall be delivered, everyone that shall be found written in the book" (Daniel 12:1). As a friend of mine often says, "the idea of the Second Coming as a freeing experience loses out in the struggle with that event as a terrible and fearsome moment." But remember the word of Jesus, "Let not your heart be troubled. Ye believe in God, believe also in me...I will come again and receive you unto myself that where I am, there ye may be also" (John 14:1, 3). What an expectation: freedom in the presence of God and eternal togetherness! James Oppenheim writes about it:

> *"Machinery is enough for the scientist,*
> *and beauty is enough for the poet.*
> *But in the hearts of men and women, and in*
> *The thirsty hearts of little children*
> *There is hunger, and there is an unappeasable*
>   *longing*
> *For a Father and for the love of a Father."*

The end of the world is no longer a bad dream. Informed scientists and reputable economists are now predicting that a combination of factors will make world catastrophe inevitable. As Dr. Carl Sagan reflected, "We have placed our civilization and our species in jeopardy".[23] What shall we do? Anyone who suggests a spiritual remedy for our contemporary sickness is looked upon with suspicion. We'll try any cure but religion. Divine help is the last resort; but surely we have come to the time of last resorts and the wise thing to do is to think and act positively. As Joseph Auslander appeals:

> *"World, oh world of muddled men,*
> *Seek the peace of God again;*
> *In the humble faith that kneels,*
> *In the hallowed Word that heals;*
> *In the hope that answers doubt,*
> *Love that drives the darkness out.*
> *Frantic, frightened, foolish men,*
> *Take God by that hand again."*

Remember, the world's end is God's opportunity and earth's new beginning.

VI
RED STAIRS TO THE SUN

> *"Why are men willing to attach significance only to grim and painful historical events, but not to the new beginning that God has provided in Jesus Christ for the salvation of the human family?"* —Adolph Köberle *(German theologian)*

The ancients had been here. A record of Ramses II of Egypt boasted of his campaigns against the Edomites of Seir. The tablets of Tiglath Pileser, the Assyrian king, the monuments of Esarhaddon, and the records of Nebuchadnezzar of Babylon mention the Edomites and their wonderful city. Though ancient authors had written of it, like so many other dead cities, the location of Petra had been forgotten.

In 1812 a young Anglo-Swiss adventurer, John Lewis Buckhardt, discovered the ruins as he was journeying from Damascus to Cairo. He contrived to get into the city by disguising himself as an Arab and pretended he was going to sacrifice a goat to Aarun (Aaron), on top of a mountain nearby which is supposed to be the site of the patriarch's tomb. Later, an English poet from Newgate, the Reverend John Burgon, following his visit to Petra in 1845 described it in these memorable words:

> *"Match you this wonder, save in Eastern clime,*
> *A rose-red city, half as old as time."*

Robin Fedden, in his book on Syria describes "the broiling rocks of Petra" and the "leopards and deserted Nabataean temples." I wanted to see it.

The road to Petra leads south from Amman in Jordan through an inhospitable land devoid of water or vegetation and virtually deserted apart from buses loaded with pilgrims returning from Mecca. Finally, after a four-hour drive we arrive at *Wadi Musa* (the Valley of Moses), an

An Adventure into Discovery

engaging little village of square mud huts and green terraces. I declined to ride into Petra on a horse preferring rather to negotiate the rugged path on the safety of my own two feet. The equestrian offerings were not famed Arabian stallions but rather staid old nags. I recalled Mark Twain's visit to this place and the name he gave his steed, "Baalbek." Why was the creature given such an unlikely title? He replied, "Because it was a magnificent ruin!"

After a one-hour walk we reached the red sandstone mountains which form a natural barrier around the old city, enclosing it on all sides. Entrance to the city through this mountain barrier is obtained through a few narrow rock gorges. The one we used winds its way through a torturous defile for about 8,000 feet between towering cliffs, deep red and copper, ochre and violet. The Arabs call it *Siq*, meaning "cleft." The gorge, nowhere wider than sixty feet, and in most places not more than twenty feet, has perpendicular walls stretching up to 160 feet. Sometimes the high overhead rocks nearly join, and a dramatic shaft of sunlight knifing down between them illuminates the trail. An occasional fountain of green and golden vines or an oleander bush spurts from a crevice in the rock face, a hidden deposit of moisture giving it life. Other than the sound of the horses' hooves scattering the gravel there is no sound at all.

This long, narrow entrance was formerly paved, and artificial channels led the water of the *Wadi Musa* into Petra, but most of the masonry has been swept away in the course of centuries, and the going is now rather rough. Ambling through the narrow haunting *Siq*, I remember a tragedy of a few years back, when a flash flood poured through the twisted gorge, trapping a party of travelers and drowning them all. Happily, the danger no longer exists since the Jordanian government has reconstructed a Nabatean dam to control the flow of water. It can readily been seen that a city surrounded by high mountains like Petra, which could be reached only through narrow clefts more than a mile long, could easily be defended.

After walking through the *Siq* with its menacing cliffs and chilly darkness, seeing nothing but the colorful rock walls and a blue ribbon of sky over us, the passage suddenly widens. A flood of sunlight is admitted by the gap in the mountain and in awed amazement we see before us a strange and picturesque structure, the *El Khazneh*, a magnificent temple over sixty feet high, carved like a cameo from the sandstone cliff face.

Stunned, I turned around and saw the slot in the mountainside from which I had just emerged. Through that same passageway came the inhabitants who built a city intended to last forever. You know it, although you cannot see it, and you sense the presence of two thousand fifty years. I sat and reviewed the history of the site.

The city, because of its location in the midst of the rocks, was first called by the Semitic name *Sela*, "Rock." In later times it received the Greek name Petra, which has the same meaning. The earliest records concerning the inhabitants of this area from the Bible, which provides the information that the Horites lived in this region before the Edomites (Deuteronomy 2:12). Known from non-biblical records of Mesopotamia and Egypt as Hurrians, the Horites were found in the early second millennium B.C. throughout the Near East, from northern Mesopotamia down to the border of Egypt. Later Esau, Jacob's twin brother, settled in the area south of the Dead Sea, and the Edomites, his descendants, gradually replaced the Hurrians, being in possession of this area when the children of Israel left Egypt.

After having traversed the desert country of Sinai for many years, Moses requested from the Edomites permission to pass through their country. He promised to use only "the king's highway" (Numbers 20:17), a road that had been used from time immemorial between Damascus and western Arabia. The Edomites refused this request and threatened to fight against the Israelites if they would try to travel through their country. Thus Moses was forced to lead his people through the inhospitable desert country surrounding the land of Edom. This unfriendly act was the beginning of a deep-seated hatred between the two nations which occasionally broke out in open warfare. Hence we read that Saul fought against the Edomites (1 Samuel 14:47), while David subdued them and garrisoned their country (2 Samuel 8:14). Solomon also ruled them but when the kingdom of Judah fell into weakness, the Edomites became independent again (1 Kings 11).

The Edomites were later driven out of their mountainous territory by the Arabian Nabataeans. Settling in southern Palestine, they were once more subjugated by the Jews in the time of the Maccabees, whose rules forced them to accept the Jewish religion and its rites. From that time on the Arab Nabataeans occupied the former country of the Edomites and made Petra, the rich caravan city, their capital, controlling from this stronghold much of the territory of Transjordania, from the Gulf of Aqaba in the south to Damascus in the north.

Since the Nabataeans occupied a favorable strategic position, they were able for centuries to control the desert roads between Arabia and Egypt, as well as those leading from western Arabia to Anatolia, Syria and Mesopotamia. Caravans traveling on these roads had to pay taxes to the Nabataeans, who became in this way wealthy and were thus able to build fine palaces, temples, theatres and tombs in their capital city. When the Romans became masters of the eastern Mediterranean world they coveted this territory for its wealth and strategic value, and after conquering Petra made it part of the Roman Empire. However, the story of Petra was not that of Carthage, and although now a Roman province, she again began to prosper and some of the finest monuments were built in that era.

The best preserved of all these is *El Khazneh*, meaning "The Treasury." Emerging from the crepuscular twisting chasm, the traveler is confronted by this structure with its double tier of pediments and Corinthian columns.

Red Stairs to the Sun

Sheltered by overhanging rock, it is the best preserved of all the monuments of Petra. It seems to have been a temple dedicated by the Nabataeans to Isis, an Egyptian goddess. Built in Greek style, it has no great importance to the archaeologist. Three doors lead to rock-hewn halls and chambers. The central door is nearly thirty feet high and fifteen feet wide. The upper story is solid, but there are more columns, and in the center is a circular lantern with a mutilated statue of Isis in the front. The columns and porticos of the Treasury, as they are in all the tombs, are not built but carved into the rock face. When the sun strikes the rose-red sandstone it glows as though lighted from within. The urn that tops the central circular ornamentation of the upper pediment is bullet marked—the assaults by those who hoped to shatter the building and release the treasure that legend claims is buried there. Actually, no treasure has ever been found in the Nabataean tombs as it was in those of the Egyptians.

From the clearing in which "The Treasury" stands the track narrows, lined on either side by tombs, opening out again when it reaches the theater. The theater was built by the Romans who, after their arrival, gave the tombs in their way short shrift. Probably their philosophy was: we're living; they're dead; let's get on with it!

The Treasury, Petra

From the theater onward along the Roman road flanked by a few standing columns, past the remains of a triumphal arch, the high walls diminish, the valley widens into an undulating plain a mile long, three-quarters of a mile wide, ringed with low hills. Here and there rises an outcropping of high rock formation.

The conception of Petra was unusual and its execution extraordinary. For the most part, the tombs were carved

An Adventure into Discovery

high up into the faces of the cliffs, and it must have required not only imagination and skill but vacuum cup feet to negotiate the perpendicular façades and achieve the sculptors' design. At times one thinks the cliffs must surely be marble because of the markings: navy streaks of blue and white and purple. In reality, it is the natural coloring of much of the sandstone, and when the afternoon sun bathes the great western facade it glows like a rose-garden.

However, I came to Petra for more serious reasons than merely to admire the colorful facades of Petra. Two mountaintops inside the city have connection with Old Testament history. One is Umm el Biyara, the rocky mountain on which the Edomite capital once stood, and the other is Jebel el-Madhbah (*mountain of the altar*), on which an ancient high place of sacrifice is found.

Although nearly two thousand monuments of the Nabataean Petra are of indescribable charm and beauty to the lover of ancient art, they date from the Greek and Roman periods, not from the time of the Edomites. The earlier ruins of the Edomites are found on the top of a high mountain, called by the Arabs *Umm el Biyara*, "Mother of Cisterns," because of the great number of cisterns in which the Edomites once collected and stored rain water.

I could also clearly understand the words of the prophet Jeremiah who, when speaking of the Edomites and undoubtedly of *Sela*, their capital, said, "O thou that dwellest in the clefts of the rock, that holdest the height of the hill: ...make thy nest as high as the eagle" (Jeremiah 49:16). No words could better describe the favorable location of this rock city. However, Jeremiah saw that its impregnable position would not save it from destruction. He forecast that the city "shall be perpetual wastes" and that all visitors would be "astonished" by what they saw! (v. 17). Obadiah similarly predicted, "And there shall not be any remaining of the house of Esau!' (Obadiah 18), and Joel and Isaiah vividly described its fate as a "desolate wilderness" and "stones of emptiness" (Joel 3:19; Isaiah 34:11).

Yet despite these prophecies, as we have already seen, Petra continued to flourish. Although the peak of their prosperity and power was probably from the first century B.C. to the end of the first century A.D., it is easy to understand that the future of the Petrans was integrally linked with their Roman allies. As Rome declined, so did Petra. For anguished years the city struggled to stay alive. Then, the final die was cast when a new caravan route was opened up, a route that bypassed Petra in favor of Palmyra, far to the north. So when caravans took other routes between the Orient and Europe, and especially after the sea lane around Africa was discovered, caravan traffic through Nabataean territory dried up.

This was the blow that cut the proud city to the heart, and Petra's lifeblood—her commerce—began to drain away. The people deserted their homes, their temples, their theaters and structures that once throbbed with beauty now sank into dust and decay, as Petra, the power and the glory of the Middle East, became, in fulfillment of the Word of God, a lifeless valley scattered with the rose-red remnants of a vanished civilization.

So the city was deserted and forgotten, and for centuries Petra seemed to be a legendary city like Atlantis, known only from records of the past. It wasn't until Burckhardt discovered the lost city that anyone realized that such a picturesque site lay only 100 miles south of Jerusalem.

After having climbed to the top of *Umm el Biyara*, I had the desire to climb another of Petra's mountains, where the best-preserved ancient "high place" of the Middle East is found. Nearby the cleft entrance to the city, a narrow stairway hewn out of rock ascends to the summit. After a torturous ascent of one mile we reach the top of Zibb'Atuf. It is one of those open-air sanctuaries frequently mentioned in the Bible as "high places" (See 1 Kings 14:23; 15:14; 22:43, etc.)

An Adventure into Discovery

Reaching this "sacred" area from the south, we came first upon a water tank eight by ten feet wide and three feet deep, cut out from the rock as is everything else in this place. Rock-hewn channels once drained rain water into the tank, which was probably used for ritual ablution purposes. Just behind the tank there is a large court, forty-seven feet long and twenty feet wide, with a raised platform in the middle, the spot where the victims—animals and humans—were sacrificed.

On the north side is a low rock bench used for the preparation of the victims before they were taken to the rock-hewn altar, which is standing on the western side. Five steps lead up to the square hearth on which the sacrifice was burnt. To the left of the altar of burnt offerings is another circular altar, upon which the libation offerings of wine and oil were poured out.

Not far from this court stands two big obelisk-like pillars, cult objects found in connection with every ancient high place. They were formed by cutting away the surrounding rock. The purpose of these pillars is not entirely clear; either they represent the rays of the sun and were worshipped as sun pillars, or they were symbols of fertility.

Obviously the inhabitants of Petra regarded the high place as their chief place of worship and while it was too small for public services it was probably intended for priestly acts of oblation and propitiation. The rock hewn channels, the altar of burnt offering, the place of sacrifice, speak for themselves. Like the rest of the people in the Near East the Nabataeans were obsessed with guilt and sought to relieve it by sacrificial worship.

Actually, animal sacrifice appears to be a characteristic of all ancient religions. Most of the literature of the Greeks, the Egyptians, the Chinese, the Hindus and the traditions of many nations agree that man at a very early stage in history recognized that he could not approach God in his own righteousness. He was too sinful. He needed a sacrifice, a substitute to atone for him. "Sacrifice," writes Professor E. O. James, "involves the destruction of a victim to maintain or restore a right relationship between man and the sacred order by effacing a bond of union with the divinity to whom it is offered: or to 'cover,' 'wipe out,' neutralize or carry away evil and guilt contracted wittingly or unwittingly".[24]

This definition sounds rather academic. Put in simpler terms the basic aim of sacrifices was to establish a union between man and God and to restore that union when it was broken. It did not matter who the worshipper was—Egyptian or Jew, Phoenician or Nabataean, the purpose was the same; and in order for sacrifice to be effective, the offerer had to be identified with the victim. This was usually symbolized by laying hands upon it. Then it was necessary for something to be forfeited or destroyed in order to establish a right relationship with the source of strength. Life must be given in order to promote and preserve life. "The central point, however, is not the slaughter but the application of the blood and the sharing of the life."[25]

Salvation by substitutionary death was central to Israel's sanctuary system. On the bronze-covered altar of sacrifice, innocent animals died in a pathetic, heartbreaking ritual that illustrated God's mercy in providing for the atonement of man's sin. It came down to this: the person offering a sacrifice would bring a ceremonially clean animal to the priest and lay his hands on the animal's head. Then and there the animal would be slaughtered. It was an ugly, public drama that showed God's willingness to let an innocent animal die in the place of its guilty human sacrificer. Such a system taught men the way of salvation before Jesus, the Lamb of God (John 1:9) paid the ultimate sacrifice. "Thy way, O God, is in the sanctuary," exclaimed the psalmist (Psalms 77:13).

This practice has a long history. Just after Adam and Eve sinned, God initiated the process of blood sacrifice to bring home the reality of what sin means. He instituted this violent object lesson to illustrate a plan that would

An Adventure into Discovery

enable Him to be merciful to the offender through its ultimate fulfillment.

It was a practice that was controversial from the beginning. Consider the argument between Cain and Abel: Apparently God had told them that they must approach Him on the basis of blood sacrifice. This irritated Cain; after all, he worked the soil. His pride and self respect was challenged to think that God would favor an animal sacrifice more than a grain, vegetable or fruit offering. After all, an offering of his own harvest would not only give him a chance to sacrifice the work of his own hands, it would also be cleaner and less violent. Cain tried. God didn't "buy it." The blood sacrifice of Abel was accepted. Cain refused to offer a blood sacrifice, and ironically, he shed the blood of his own brother.

Men are still divided over the issue of blood sacrifice. It seems crude and detestable to some. They resent the idea of having to come to God through the principle of blood sacrifice, fulfilled for us in Christ, rather than on the basis of their own work and show of faith. They resent the whole idea of the Lamb of God, spoken so clearly by the Old Testament sacrifices. Yet in the process they miss the fact that this blood sacrifice finally would pay for any of our sins, and that this Lamb of God would actually rise from the dead to prove it.

As the tabernacle so beautifully shows us, that blood sacrifice is where a walk with God begins. It represents that act of God's unmerited favor by which He accepts us because His Son paid the price for our guilt and sin.

As I climbed the stairs that lead to Petra's high place, I thought of altars I had seen in Iraq, India, Lebanon, Egypt, Mexico, the South Pacific Islands and Jerusalem. Everywhere men have been aware that their relationship with God has been ruptured and they are responsible. The guilty conscience is a universal phenomenon. There is more to the Bible story of the Fall than Eve and the apple! Beneath the surface of religiosity is the common recognition that something has gone wrong we shall have to pay for, because we are to blame.

Always there is the risk that guilt will get the better of us. The simple truth behind the sacrificial idea has often been distorted until God is envisaged as one who has to be appeased and bargained with, a terrifying monster who delights in sacrifices and enjoys slaughter. Witness, for instance, the sacrificial perversion of the Aztecs in the 15th century A.D. and the Hebrews during the reign of King Solomon in the 10th century B.C.

With the Aztecs, the Sun God developed an insatiable appetite for human sacrifice and his worship depended upon and necessitated ceaseless war—wars that were fought solely to feed the gods. For Xipe-totec, God of Spring, victims were flayed alive and their skins donned by officiating priests.

> "At this feast they killed all the prisoners, men, women and children. The owners of the prisoners handed them over to the priests at the foot of the temple, and they pulled them by the hair up the steps; and if they did not wish to go they were dragged to the block of stone where they were to kill them, and taking from each one his heart, they hurled the bodies down the steps where the priests flayed them. After they had been flayed ... they dismembered them and sent a limb to Montezuma to eat, and the rest they shared amongst the priests and relatives".[26]

As for numbers, one record says that 20,000 quivering hearts were offered during the dedication of the Great Temple at Tenochtitlan.

The sacrificial cult reached terrible excesses amongst the Canaanites. Lenormant testifies: "No other people ever rivaled them in the mixture of bloodshed and debauchery with which they thought to honor the Deity".[27] Archaeologists who have excavated several Canaanite towns spoke of an almost Aztec-like disregard of the value of human life and found evidence of the wholesale massacre and sacrifice of infants. The Hebrew religion became so influenced by these practices it assimilated all the grosser aspects of paganism. "They caused their sons and daughters to pass through the fire and used divinations and enchantments and sold themselves to do evil." (2 Kings 17:17)

King Solomon promoted the animal sacrifices on such a colossal scale it has seldom been approximated anywhere. At the dedication of his temple in Jerusalem, twenty-two thousand oxen, a hundred and twenty thousand sheep were slain. (2 Chronicles 7:5)

Yet despite its perversion, the sacrificial idea is capable of developing into the noblest of any religious acts—the utter abandonment of the worshipper to the purpose of the divine Being, the continuous separation for one's shortcomings, the cathartic effect of confession and the release of forgiveness. Even at the crudest level, sacrificial rituals kept alive the thought of a God who sees and a God who makes demands upon his worshippers. These are valuable insights that modern man is apt to forget. Yet at the bottom of his psychical disturbances is the same sense of guilt which gave rise to the first act of sacrifice.

The sense of estrangement is just as strong as ever. We are still at war with ourselves, conscious of the gap between ideals and practice, between what is and what ought to be. The frontier between the technology, morality and metaphysics is not easily defined. Call it what we may in twentieth century terms, complex neurosis, fixation, evolutionary lag, social maladjustment or just plain ignorance, we are still plagued by the same old fears, tortured with the same old doubts, overwhelmed with the same old inadequacies. Despite our bravados we are sick at heart and troubled in mind. As Celia Copplestone says to the psychiatrist in T. S. Eliot's play:

> "It's not the feeling of anything I've done, which I might get away from or of anything in me I could get rid of but of emptiness, or failure towards someone or something outside of myself. And I feel I must atone—is that

the word? Can you treat a patient for such a state of mind?"

The Old Testament prophet Micah provides an up-to-date answer:

> "Wherewith shall I come before the Lord, and bow myself before the high God? Shall I come before him with burnt offerings, with calves of a year old? Will the Lord be pleased with thousands of rams or with ten thousands of rivers of oil? Shall I give my firstborn for my transgression, the fruit of my body for the sin of my soul? He hath showed thee, O man, what is good; and what doth the Lord require of thee, but to do justly, and to love mercy, and to walk humbly with thy God?"—Micah 6:6-8

God Himself would provide a lamb who would end the daily round of sacrifices and offerings once and for all. (See 1 Peter 2:24; Colossians 2:14):

> "Yet on himself he bore our sufferings, our torments he endured
> He was pierced for our transgressions, tortured for our iniquities
> The chastisement he bore is health for us and by his scourging we are healed."
> (See Isaiah 53)

Soon the Greeks were questioning the motives of sacrifice too. Aristophanes was laughing at the kind of antics priests go up to ensure the favor of the gods. Peithetairos, in the Birds, builds a city in the clouds, and so cuts off the smoke of the sacrifices from the gods who begins to feel starved and send an embassy to arrange a treaty with the new republic. The well-known Platonic dialogue "Euthyphro" represents Socrates as asking,

> "But what is the object of sacrifice? Does it really have an effect? And in any case what sort of deities are those who have to be haggled with, and whom we even try to cheat by substituting a cheap offering for a more expensive one in the hope that they won't notice the difference?"

Things were moving to a climax by the first century B.C. In Judea, the Essenes had disassociated themselves from the Temple in Jerusalem entirely, and had set up a community down by the Dead Sea where Atonement was made by prayer, through the "offering of the lips." They believed the sacrifices of God are "a broken spirit, a broken and a contrite heart" and were a matter of inward spirituality rather than outward ceremony. Even without sacrificial rites, a holy life was endowed with expiatory and sanctifying value.[28]

Then came Jesus with the news that "God loved the world so much he gave his only son that everyone who has faith in him may not die but have eternal life. It was not to judge the world that God sent his son into the world but that through him the world might be saved." (John 3:16, 17)

However, the full meaning of his words was not appreciated until the crucifixion. Then Christians realized that what had been symbolized in the sacrificial system of the sanctuary as well as what the prophets had said was fulfilled in him in a remarkable way. He had died at the height of the Passover season and on Mount Moriah, the place where Abraham said God himself would provide a lamb. What is more, at the very moment Jesus bowed his head and gave up the ghost, the curtain separating the Holy from the Most Holy place in the Temple was torn into shreds from top to bottom (Matthew 27:50, 51). No longer did men need to bring lambs, for the Lamb of God "slain from the foundation of the world" had been sacrificed (1 Peter 1:18-19).

> *"The Lamb has died*
> *Upon*
> *An altar lifted high*
> *A rough hewn wooden one*
> *Stretched against*
> *The sky.*
> *The Lamb has died*
> *Before*
> *This little world began*

He made the fateful choice
And gave Himself
To man.

The Lamb has died
To save
Me from the guilt of sin
Has made the sacrifice
And given peace
Within.

The Lamb,
The Lamb,
The Bleeding Lamb
Has died."—Christina Rossetti

The implications of His sacrifice are now unmistakably clear. Jesus is the only answer to the sin problem. No other substitute than the Lamb of God can save man from the burden of his guilt and the penalty of sin (Acts 4:12). Jesus is the only one to whom I should confess my sin. No other person can assume my guilt and promise me pardon. He alone has power to forgive men their trespasses (Colossians 2:13). While many sacrifices were made in the ancient temple ritual, Christ's one offering cancels all sin and that sacrifice never needs to be repeated (*Hebrews* 10:14; 7:25, 28; 10:1, 2, 10-12). Furthermore, Jesus is man's only Mediator. There is no need for any earthly priesthood today. In the Old Testament system, the benefits of the substitutionary sacrifice were fully applied to the sinner when the blood was sprinkled in the Sanctuary (*Leviticus* 4:7, 17, 20, 34, 35). Christ was a sacrifice before He was a priest. He died as sacrifice and ascended to heaven, where as priest He ministers the benefits of His sacrifice (Hebrews 9:11-14) and shares with us the spoils of His victory (Hebrews 2:15-17; 4:15, 16). Christ, our great High Priest, is our only priest (1 Timothy 2:5). In the Jewish temple there were many priests—since the Cross there is but one and He lives forever to make intercession for us (Hebrews 7:11, 23-25).

Finally, the bargain basis has completely gone. God was seen as no respecter of persons. He makes His rain fall on the just and unjust alike and offers forgiveness without charge, He Himself having paid the price. His gifts are not offered according to man's deserts, but according to His grace. He gives continuously lest anyone should think His loving nature changes. This is all part of Christ's legacy to the world. These timeless truths about the character of God and His concern for mankind are made known in Christ, and provide the only cure for the psychical disorders that distress modern man.

The Red Stairs of Petra reach beyond Zibb'Atuf with its obelisks and altars. It is interesting to think that Nabataean priests like the Levites at Jerusalem were still offering their sacrifices when Jesus was carrying His cross; but not even the impenetrable Siq, with its deep ravine and narrow entrance and lofty precipices, could keep the good news out. The gospel reached Petra as it turned the world upside down. A Byzantine church built during the fifth century, a Greek inscription from A.D. 447 in the so-called Urn Tomb and crosses carved on dozens of doorways testify to the presence of a Christian community. We know that some of the most impressive Nabataean temples like *El Deir* were adapted for Christian usage, for Christian crosses are painted and scored all over the walls.

When the day breaks, the shadows flee away.

VII

THE STRANGE FATE OF MASADA

"If men could learn from history, what lessons it might teach us! But passion and party blind our eyes, and the light which experience gives is a lantern on the stern which shines only on the waves behind us."
—Samuel Taylor Coleridge

Climbing in the desert heat to the lofty rock fortress brooding over the barren Judean wilderness and the salty flats of the Dead Sea, I recently set foot on one of the great archaeological finds of modern times—Masada. (The name Masada is a Hellenized form of the original Hebrew *Metsada* or *Metsuda*, meaning "stronghold.") This boat-shaped rock, 1,350 feet high, is among the most pulse-stirring places in the world. It is encompassed with valleys so abrupt such as no animal can walk upon them. There are valleys of so great a magnitude that the eye cannot measure their depths.

This rock, once the refuge of David from the murderous designs of King Saul, was first fortified during the Maccabean revolt against the Seleucid successors of Alexander the Great in the second century B.C. And here, "almost 2,000 years ago," my Israeli guide said, "the strangest and most heroic last stand in history occurred." Then, leading me among the ruins, he related the dramatic story.

The Jewish historian, Flavius Josephus, has in fact described these events, which have left their imprint upon the landscape forever, and through them, the Rock Masada has become an Israeli national symbol of independence and heroism.

The history of Masada goes back before Christ to the days when Herod was king over the desert in Jerusalem. Jerusalem has had the misfortune of being the most "blessed" of cities. Blessed to the Muslims, as the spot from which Mohammed left earth for heaven. Blessed to the Christian for the many places within and about it which evoke Christ's ministry and passion, and blessed to the Jews as the place where Jehovah promised Abraham and his descendents preeminence in His sight.

As a result, Jerusalem has been throughout history a city of contention, torn between opposing faiths, the center of destructive holy wars. Crowded within its walls, places of intense religious significance stand side by side. The "wailing wall" is the most poignant relic of Jewry, yet it is nothing more than a fragment of the platform of Solomon's temple which was destroyed by the Romans in A.D. 70. The temple itself had been the focus of the Jewish faith ever since its foundation on the site. Destroyed and rebuilt again and again, finally it was replaced with celebrated magnificence by Herod the Great in the first decade B.C.

The new splendor was entirely due to Herod himself—a moody king who ruled over the Jews for 33 years, up to the time of the birth of Christ. Nominally, Herod's religion was Judaism, but his family was originally foreign and Gentile; but the Jewish nation had so isolated itself from its neighbors by its tradition of exclusivity, that it became Herod's great ambition to draw his kingdom into the brilliant mainstream of Greek and Roman civilization from which his people stood aloof.

For his numerous subjects Herod erected many a splendid building as well as the Great Temple. There was a theater and Greek performers for the drama. There was the hippodrome for the less cultured, but then both horseracing and the stage were considered evil and wicked by the Jew. The sad fact was that, in the eyes of his Jewish subjects, Herod never seemed to put a foot right. His preoccupation with foreign tastes was abhorrent to them. His court spoke not Hebrew, but Greek; even the coinage carried Greek lettering. So, hated by his own people as "the usurper," and more especially for his non-Jewish background, the most essential building to guarantee Herod's

The Strange Fate of Masada

rule was the fortress which menaced and controlled the whole city. To add insult to injury, it was called "Via Antonia" after his libertine Roman friend, Mark Antony, and it was manned by the Roman army, Herod's allies, against his own subjects, the Jews. Thus, afraid of his own people, afraid of international enemies like Cleopatra, the scheming queen of Egypt, whom Herod feared might get Judea from Antony as a gift, Herod devoted much of his activities to the construction of defensive fortifications for his own security.

Perfect for its difficult access, its remoteness and the fact that it controlled the vital southeastern approach to the kingdom, there was no place better suited for a stronghold than the rock Masada.

Masada

In order to render the natural inaccessibility of the place completely impregnable, Herod encircled the summit with a stone wall three-quarters of a mile in circumference. The few perilous routes to the top were blocked by 45 gates. The most vulnerable approaches were commanded by 37 tall towers. In case of siege, he built 15 large storehouses and filled them with weapons and armor, of permanent stocks of corn-wine oil and dried fruit, enough for a great many people for a very long time.

Perhaps the most amazing feature of Herod's refuge was the ingenious way in which the rock was riddled with enormous cisterns for the storage of water. Rain collected on the hills opposite; it poured down the valleys and was diverted across the ravine on an aqueduct constructed like a bridge. This brought the water rushing down this channel so that the maximum current could be directed into the cistern. When rains come to Masada, they come in a flood, so it would have been a matter of only a few hours when a whole series of eight cisterns would have been filled. These were made economically. First of all Herod's quarrymen cut them out of the living rock and used the excavated stone as building material. They were then lined with plaster—which is still in good condition—in order to prevent the water from seeping back into the rock. In this way they managed to convert quarry into cistern and thus store hundreds of thousands of gallons up here on Masada.

While he was insuring his stronghold against siege, the pleasure-loving Herod still thought of his luxury. So there was even a swimming pool installed for the king and his guests, showing how prodigal he could afford to be with his water even though there is no natural spring up here at all.

The administrative center for ceremonials and a palace for audiences were on the western side of the mountain. It, too, had its inevitable bath house, making use yet again of the element which Masada lacked but which Herod had made so abundant.

The details that are preserved show what a fine place it must have been. For all Herod knew, events may force him to spend the rest of his life up here, so he spared no expense to make it attractive to the eye as well as comfortable with fine mosaic floors. But they are all geometric patterns for he still felt obliged to avoid the repre-

The Strange Fate of Masada

sentation of men and animals which was forbidden by Jewish law.

Outside the palace there were many more buildings to house his family and his staff and the soldiers to protect him. Josephus records:

> "The king reserved the top of the hill which had a lot of fat soil and better mould than any valley for agriculture, that such as committed themselves to this fortress might not even there be quite destitute for food."

Finally, on the extreme northern tip of this gaunt and beating rock, Herod had a magnificent three-tier villa constructed. Enough of the colonnades and mosaics survive to enable us to visualize the splendor of the original place—almost incredible in that desolate environment and on an eminence so difficult of access. As I descended the steps from the topmost terrace to the bottom, a distance of well over a hundred feet, and then climb back up (much more slowly, with frequent compulsory stops to admire the views), I marveled more and more at how such a feat of construction could have been performed in those distant days; but it was here, in seclusion and safety, that Herod took his pleasures.

Actually, he hardly used it himself at all. His Roman friends, with their powerful armies, preserved him from the dangers which he feared so much until he died in 4 B.C., leaving his citadel to a succession of Roman garrisons.

However, after Herod's death, Roman rule grew harsher as Jewish intransigence towards it increased, until finally the mixture boiled over into a disastrous revolt, and in A.D. 66, Rome dispatched an army of 60,000 which, after four years of ruthless warfare, crushed the uprising. The Romans then sacked and burnt Jerusalem, tossed children into the flames and shipped off some of the survivors to Rome, where they were paraded through the streets in chains.

An Adventure into Discovery

Almost 100 years had passed since Masada had been fortified and provisioned by Herod. By now the rock was occupied by a sleepy garrison of Roman soldiers stationed up there on the top. Thus by A.D. 66 the stage was set for Masada's greatest moment of drama.

All of a sudden, a ragged group of Jews rushed the fortress and captured it. As the Roman army was busy elsewhere, they were able to hold Masada without opposition for six years. They were not soldiers, these new possessors of the rock, but religious folk. They belonged to a sect of strict Orthodox Jews called Zealots, the last of the most dedicated rebels against the Romans under their most fanatical leader, Eleazer ben Ya'ir.

Herod had not planned his fortress for nearly as many people who had joined the Zealots. They subdivided his fine buildings with dismal jerry-built partitions. Herod's sumptuous palaces became the headquarters of the movement and the residence of the leaders. They made holes in the mosaic floors for their crude cooking pots. The rock took on the appearance of a shantytown, a slum. Yet the signs of their religious life appear everywhere, representing the spirit which infected every one of them. They constructed their basins for ritual ablutions—essential to the Jewish faith. They built a synagogue, the earliest that survives. No doubt their devotions occupied much of the time they waited up here on Masada.

However, there were more practical matters to attend to, preparing the walls against attack and armoring themselves. In this search for equipment they were lucky, for Josephus tells us:

> "There was also found here a great quantity of weapons of war which had been treasured up by Herod and was sufficient for 10,000 men. There was cast iron and brass and tin which show he had taken great pains to have all things ready here for the great occasion."

Thus armed by Herod's hundred-year-old store of weapons and armored by spiritual cleanliness, the Zealots sat on the rock and waited for Masada's greatest occasion of all; for six years they waited.

They had heard, with loud lamentations, of the fall of Jerusalem in A.D. 70. Then rumors came of the collapse of the scattered outposts of the rebellion, one by one. Finally, those on Masada were the only ones left. Perhaps they thought they would be left alone there in such a remote and forbidding part of the country; but Rome was not in the habit of turning its back on rebellious and troublesome subjects.

Then one day, late in A.D. 72, came the Romans. Over the hills and down the valleys came the army, marching. One legion it was, the tenth, a body of as many as 5,000 battle-scarred well-trained troops. Mostly they would have been infantry, but they brought their specialized arms as well: the artillery, a little cavalry and, of course, the engineers who were going to be so useful on this job. Then there would have been the *auxilia*—locally raised troops supporting the legion, of about the same strength. The entire force was commanded by Flavius Silva, Procurator of Judea. One of those "no-nonsense-get-on-with-it" Roman officers who had made the name of the Roman army so feared throughout the ancient world. All-in-all, some 10-15,000 trained men, plus countless prisoners to do the "donkey-work," marched toward Masada.

The Zealots watched from the summit as within a few hours the Romans laid out their regulation square camp. Silva's own camp lay right under the summit so the Zealots could watch every move the Romans made. Silva knew that he had to contain his enemy as well as threaten him, so he extended his siege works outwards from his base to encircle the entire rock. When the work was finished, Masada was encircled by an impenetrable ring. Having contained his enemy, Silva now built a stupendous ramp, a thousand feet high, and launched a massive assault from the West. The wall on the summit was breached. The sun was low in the west, and with victory imminent, the Romans retreated to their camp to prepare for an all-out attack the next day.

As flames raced along Masada's ramparts, Eleazer ben Ya'ir called the leaders of his besieged band together for a conference of despair. "Daybreak will end our resistance," he told them. He spoke long and persuasively and in the end everybody agreed to abide by his last desperate decision.

> "While our hands are still at liberty and have a sword in them, let them then be subservient to us in our glorious design. Let us die before we become slaves under our enemies and let us go out of this world in company with our wives and our children in a state of freedom. Let them say that we chose death rather than slavery."

Moved by Eleazer's fervent appeal, his companions vowed mass suicide for the beleaguered band of 960 Zealots. Each man, having tenderly bade his own family farewell, killed them. Josephus eloquently describes the final grim chapter:

> "They chose 10 men by lot, to slay all the rest...when the 10 had slain them all, they cast lots for themselves, choosing one to kill the other nine. Then, after the one who remained had assured himself that all were dead, he set fire to the royal palace, and with his full strength drove his sword into his body."

The next morning the trumpeting 10th legion launched its confident assault. But instead of the expected bitter resistance, the Romans found no one, but a terrible solitude and perfect silence—smoldering ruins. Then two terrified women and a group of five children crept out of the underground caverns and told what had happened. Disbelieving the magnitude of the deed, the Romans did not give easy attention to the women. Quickly cutting their way through fire and debris, they came within the palace and so met with the multitude of the slain, but could take no pleasure in the fact, though it were done to their enemies.

The Strange Fate of Masada

"They could not but wonder at the courage of their resolution, and at the immovable contempt of death which so great a number of them had shown."

Silva marched his army away. The revolt was broken after a nine-month siege. Another job well done and another battle honor for his legion. Undoubtedly, the Zealot resistance was heroic and their mass suicide one of the defiant gestures of history.

This was not the first tragedy of Jewish history. Millennia before, the Mighty God had thundered warnings that His retributive judgments would fall with a vengeance if His people refused to submit to His sovereignty (Lev. 26:14, 17, 37, 38). Lamentably, history testifies as to how they courted the disfavor of God by their belligerent, stiff-necked, unloving indifference.

Old Testament history confirms that God had placed this people in Palestine, the crossroads of the ancient world, and provided them with every facility for becoming the greatest nation on the face of the earth. Through them the world would not only see a living revelation of what God was really like, but they would also exhibit the glorious heights to which man can attain by cooperating with the infinite purposes of a great God.

Unparalleled prosperity, both temporal and spiritual, was promised them as the reward for putting in practice the righteous and wise principles of heaven. But they failed God and "brought forth wild grapes" and thus it was, in the 6th century B.C. that Nebuchadnezzar invaded Palestine and the Jews were deported to Babylon, to learn in adversity what they had failed to learn in times of prosperity. The Babylonian Captivity was to be their last chance. Through the prophet Daniel they were assured that God would not forsake them, even in exile. The people were given the promise that they would be restored to their country, the temple would be rebuilt, and Israel would have its final opportunity as a nation to cooperate with the divine plan (Daniel 9:24-27). "Seventy weeks are decreed for your people," (NAB) Daniel forecast. Not a long term of probation, you say, but the Jews understood correctly that the 490 days represented prophetic time, thus 490 years (Ezekiel 4:6; Numbers 14:34). Almost half a millennium of time to set their house in order and prepare for the long-awaited Messiah who was to spring from their race and be born in their country.

But when would this final probation commence? According to Daniel's forecast from "the going forth of the commandment to restore and build Jerusalem." Certainly, the Babylonians issued no such decree; in fact, a hundred years were to pass before permission was granted for the Jews to return to their ancestral home. By this time Babylon had fallen and the Persians were sovereign over world affairs. A Jewish princess married the Persian King Xerxes (the biblical Ahasureus), and in 457 B.C. he issued a decree granting the Jews permission to return to Palestine and rebuild their city. The prophecy was fulfilled. Jewish probation begins.

Notice, however, the prophecy comprehended more than the destiny of Israel. It even forecast the actual time of both the Messiah's baptism and death. Sir Isaac Newton saw in this remarkable fulfillment mathematical proof establishing the divinity of Jesus Christ. The New Testament provides the historical evidence that Christ's baptism was in A.D. 27 (Luke 31). Further, Jesus recognized his baptism as a fulfillment of this prophecy when He said "the time is fulfilled" (Mark 1:14, 15). Even more striking is the remarkable specificity concerning the forecast of Christ's death and the events that were to follow. The Catholic Douay Bible on Daniel 9:26 is very explicit: "After sixty-two weeks Christ shall be slain: and the people that shall deny Him *shall not be His*." The implication was clear: with the crucifixion of Christ, the Jews would forfeit their special position as God's chosen people.

At the time of the Babylonian captivity, God had specifically assured Israel that *that* experience was not to mark the "full end" of their role as the "chosen" people (Jeremiah 4:27; 5:8; 46:28). But, when the nation rejected Christ there was no assurance of their future reinstatement. The present-day return of the Jews to Palestine and the establishment of the modern state of Israel do not imply such a reinstatement, either present or future. Whatever the Jews as a nation may do, now or in the time to come, is in no way related to the former promises made to them.

God's promises are contingent upon man's cooperation and obedience. Had Israel measured up to the noble ideal, all the promises would have been fulfilled. Yet, since God's promises are immutable, what He failed to accomplish through literal Israel would now be accomplished through the Christian Church. Jesus' verdict was clear, "The kingdom of God shall be taken from you, and given to a nation bringing forth the fruits thereof" (Matthew 21:43). Paul in Romans 9 speaking of this transition, quoting Hosea, declares, "I will call them my people, which were not my people" (Romans 9:25, 26). Israel now includes not only the physical descendants of Abraham, but all who accept Christ as Savior (Acts 10:34, 35; 11:18).

Jews as individuals are not shut out. The charter members of the Christian church were all Jews. Christianity is an extension of Judaism, and all who have faith in Christ today are accepted by God as the spiritual "seed" of Abraham are "heirs according to the promise!" (Galatians 3:9).

Coleridge questioned "If men can learn from history...." Paul responded that "whatsoever things were written afore time were written" for the "learning" of future generations (1 Corinthians 10:11). And "what lessons" can be extracted from the experience of Israel? Perhaps, at least, one: if the nation of Israel were finally cast aside for their failure to measure up to the requirements of God "how much sorer punishment" will be our portion if we tread "underfoot the Son of God" (Hebrews 10:29).

A group of men stood before the Roman governor, Pilate. He offered them a choice between two men. He said he would slay one and release the other. One was a robber, a man calloused by a life of recklessness. The other was a teacher, a physician who went about doing good. Faced with the choice between these two, that group cried out "Release unto us Barrabas!" Christ was sacrificed. A decision had been made, the consequences of which are all too evident.

Every waking moment we are composing our existence by the decisions we make. Life keeps bringing us to turning points where everything ahead will be settled. The uncertain tilt toward a yes or no may lead to widely different destinies. Harry Emerson Fosdick described a barn in the Chautauqua hills where a difference of one inch at the ridgepole decided whether the rain drop drains off to the Atlantic Ocean or the Gulf of Mexico. Robert Frost gave a memorable picture of decision when he wrote:

> *"Two roads diverged in a yellow wood*
> *And sorry I could not travel both*
> *And be one traveler, long I stood*
> *And looked down one as far as I could,*
> *To where it bent in the undergrowth;*
>
> *Then took the other, as just as fair,*
> *And having perhaps the better claim,*
> *Because it was grassy and wanted wear.*
> *Though as for that, the passing there,*
> *Had worn them really about the same,*
>
> *And both that morning equally lay*
> *In leaves no step had trodden black.*
> *Oh, I kept the first for another day!*
> *Yet knowing how way leads on to way,*
> *I doubted if I should ever come back.*
>
> *I shall be telling this with a sigh*
> *Somewhere ages and ages hence:*
> *Two roads diverged in a wood,*
> *And I—*
> *I took the one less traveled by,*
> *And that has made all the difference."*
>   —Robert Frost, *The Road Less Traveled*

VIII
ENCOUNTER AT SINAI

"History is a voice forever sounding across the centuries the laws of right and wrong. Opinions alter, manners change, creeds rise and fall, but the moral law is written on the tablets of eternity." —James Anthony Froude

The Sinai encounter, occurring sometime about 1450 B.C., looms as a landmark in the story of civilization—in the Old Testament, the chief event since the Creation and the Flood. The Israelites fled from Egypt, where they had been subjected to forced labor. With few supplies, they wandered through the desert on their way to the Promised Land. It was a slow, straggling migration, and they pitched their black goat's-hair tents wherever they found a protected site. What kept their courage up is their heroic liberator, Moses—one of the greatest, most inspiring figures of antiquity.

Of Hebrew parentage, Moses was Egyptian-born-and-educated. Having slain an overseer for beating a Hebrew slave worker, he had escaped, probably to Arabia, married, and settled, so he thought, for life; but God had chosen this athletic, knowledgeable, energetic man for other things. Speaking out of a burning bush, God ordered Moses back into Egypt to free his languishing compatriots. Moses obeyed—reluctantly—and thus became the mediator between God and Israel.

As Moses scaled Mt. Sinai, he communed with God; and God gave him two stone tablets on which He has written—with his own fingers, and "on both their sides"—the Ten Commandments.

The "Covenant," or treaty of Mt. Sinai, was an alliance. From His lofty station, the Lord offered His hand to Israel in an act of grace. He would protect His people; they would keep His law. Clearly, something of vast im-

An Adventure into Discovery

portance did happen to this people on the way to Canaan. What we are witnessing is the birth of a nation, with Moses as the founding father; the wanderers exchanged the yoke of Egypt for the yoke of God.

Henceforth, the charter of the Covenant would serve as symbol of their nationhood. An Ark, or portable receptacle, was made of gold-lead-covered wood and the two stones were laid therein. When the tribes rested, a simple framework shrine—the "Tabernacle"—was reared as temporary shelter for it. On the move, they bore the Ark before them, even into battle. Eventually, King Solomon placed it in the holy of holies of his Temple, where it was guarded by two gilded cherubim, and where only the High Priest might enter once a year; and there, presumably, the stones were broken, and disappeared, in the destruction of the Temple in 586 B.C.

Now, 3,400 years later, I wanted to visit Sinai. Astonishingly, nobody knows where this mountain is. A dramatic peak called *Djebel Musa*, or Mount Moses, near the southern tip of the peninsula, is the spot where for sixteen centuries pilgrims have made the long journey here, holding this to be Mount Sinai. Nearly half the earth's population—Christians, Muslims and Jews—honor it as the spot where Moses talked with God and brought down the Law.

The wilderness of Sinai sits like an inverted triangle between the Gulf of Aqaba and the north arm of the Red Sea. Along the Mediterranean shore runs a belt of sandy country some fifteen miles deep. A high gravel and limestone plateau stretches for 150 miles to the south of this, and at the apex of the peninsula, rising to almost 8,000 feet above sea level, is a mass of granite mountains.

This is no place for a holiday. The rainfall is scarce, the country inhospitable, and vegetation is practically non-existent. This is frontier territory, a no-man's land between Egypt and southwestern Asia. Apart from a few wandering Bedouins, nobody lives here; it's too hot, too stony and too inaccessible; and yet this stark, harsh landscape, as wild as the surface of the moon, is at the same time impressive. Who could not be affected by the loneliness of the region—the sheer grandeur of the mountains of stone, their bold peaks thrusting themselves into a copper-colored noon; sand-drifts deeper than snow; the burning, blazing sun with its penetrating and purifying heat; great fissures in rock faces cutting deep into the heart of the hills; unexpected wadis with their haze of green and honeysuckle, caper, broom and tamarisk trees; high horizons and endless ridges of red granite heaving in tumultuous waves against the sky? At night the silence is unbearable, as heaven and earth blend in a harmony of color. Then, reds, golds and browns give way to purples, indigos and eventually to black. No wonder Moses brought his people through this barren wilderness to teach them about God. The solitary wonder about the place is conducive to worship.

Amongst the Sinai ranges are the ancient copper and turquoise mines to which the Egyptians sent regular expeditions. In 1904-05 Sir Flinders Petrie investigated two of these sites, and subsequent archaeological explorations have provided us with useful information about the mineral resources of the region. Annealing, the process of relieving the stress in metal by reheating, was known ages ago. By the year 2,500 B.C. the Egyptians had discovered copper ores at places like *Serabit-el-Khadem* and were sending armed convoys of miners into the Sinai Peninsula. A well-worn copper route ran down the eastern coast of the Gulf of Suez into Wadi Magdra and it was probably this road that the Hebrews used on their trek to Mount Horeb.

Of course it is to the pages of Exodus, Numbers and Deuteronomy that we are indebted for our interest in the Sinai Peninsula. Events recorded in the first books of the Bible form the kernel of our Judeo-Christian heritage.

At last, 5,000 feet above sea level, we wind up a narrow chasm-like valley and stop by the walls of what must be one of the oldest monasteries in existence, St. Catherine's. It was built here about A.D. 340—at the foot of what was believed to be the Bible's Mount Sinai, on the exact spot where God spoke to Moses out of the burning bush. Justinian, emperor of Eastern Rome, (A.D. 527-565) founded this community in honor of St. Catherine, a Christian martyr who was tortured at the wheel and beheaded in A.D. 307. According to legend, angels carried the saint's body to the top of *Jebel Katherin*, an 8,576 foot peak two and one quarter miles southwest of *Jebel Musa*. Her bones were later found and buried in the monastery chapel.

I know of no other spot that so justifies the phrase "out of this world." Lost in this mountain cranny, far from any normal route, the monks here have largely forgotten and been forgotten by the world. A 1947 American expedition was astonished to talk with Father Pachomius, who had not set foot outside the walls in 50 years, and had never heard of World War I or II. Less than a dozen Orthodox monks continue the services of their order, caring for the buildings and practicing their devotions just as holy hermits have done for centuries. Behind the tunnel-like entrance lies a miniature town of narrow paved streets, small courts, covered passageways and whitewashed buildings. Strangely enough this is one place in the world where cross and crescent exist happily together. A mosque actually stands within the monastery walls, just a few paces away from the church's bell tower explaining the preservation of the monastery through time. This is supposed to have been built over the site of the burning bush, and the monks explain that this spot is sacred to Moslems too; they revere Moses as a prophet.

Inside the church, marble floors gleam beneath a red and gold ceiling, and on a huge gilded screen called the *iconostasis* hang some of the sacred icons. The Sinai icon collection represents the entire history of this art form. Probably we can thank Mohammed for preserving such fine paintings. When Islam conquered this part of the Near East, the monastery was completely isolated from the rest of the Christian world, so the monks of St. Catherine's were not able to obey the command of Byzantine emperors to destroy all icons on the grounds that their use constituted idolatry. Only the Sinai collection survived. Another unforgettable feature of the church is the mosaic in the chapel of the burning bush, in which Moses is depicted taking off his sandals as he waits for God.

St. Catherine's also houses the world's richest monastic library. A wealth of over 3,000 ancient manuscripts recalls 1,500 years of Christianity in texts that are written in Greek, Arabic, Syriac, Georgian, Slavonic and Ethiopic languages. Most valuable of all, single manuscripts in the book room, the famous *Codex Sinaiticus*, no longer graces the shelves. The codex is one of the oldest extant manuscripts of the Bible in existence. A German scholar, Count von Tischendorf, visited the monastery in 1844, and somehow managed to take the Sinaiticus to Russia where it remained until it was purchased by the British Museum in 1933.

Did von Tischendorf purchase the Codex, or was it stolen? For over a century experts have tried to solve this "whodunit!" of the art world. Now the monks of Sinai have produced a letter written from Tischendorf himself, dated September, 1859, in which he promises to return the manuscript to the monastery just as soon as he has completed his study of it. So the British Museum displays stolen goods!

Down in the monastery's charnel house lay the skulls of thousands of holy men who had served at St. Catherine's. Monk Stephen once guarded the way up to Mount Sinai and expressed the wish that he might always do so; but when he died in A.D. 580, his brother monks set up his skeleton, garbed in a habit, to watch over the ossuary. When a man takes vows at Sinai he remains at his post long beyond the term of his natural life, but not all who came to this sacred spot survived to die of old age. Marauders frequently sacked the tiny outpost and massacred its community. This was before the time of Justinian. Because of these marauders the monks appealed to Justinian and he responded to their petition by ordering the construction of a fortified monastery that would allow the monks sufficient protection from marauders. As late as World War I the monastery was surrounded by the Turkish army, demanding entrance. Fortunately, a messenger was able to slip out through a secret passage which surfaces in the lower garden, and warn a friendly sheik who raced across the desert all the way to a British camp on the Gulf of Suez. A detachment of soldiers arrived just in time to save the monastery.

Close by the southern wall of St. Catherine's, the mountain rears up so steeply that it keeps the monastery in shadow part of the day. The climb to the top takes two or three hours, up 3,000 steps the monks had cut in the granite. At the very top is a small, flat area rich with traditions of Moses. Here, it is said, he lived 40 days and nights, communing with God, sheltering in a small grotto. A Muslim mosque and tiny Christian chapel mark the spot. The view in all directions is stupendous: over great gulfs and deserts, and rearing peaks of granite that cast ever-longer purple shadows as the sun sinks over Africa, but from *Jebel Musa's* lofty height you can view the wide expanse of *er-Rahah*, upon which a large camp could easily have been situated. This spot is sacred. A flood of religious memories crowds the mind as one surveys the scene. Once the desolate wilderness below was dotted with tents of the twelve tribes. A vast and trembling congregation waited for the giving of the covenant as clouds shrouded Moses' sight and shut him in with Jehovah. The word spoke:

> "You have seen how I have carried you on eagles' wings and brought you here to me. If only you will listen to me and keep my covenant, then out of all peoples you shall become my special possession; for the whole earth is mine. You shall be my kingdom of priests, my holy nation."—Exodus 19:4-6.

Then all the people answered together, *"Whatever the Lord has said we will do."* The earth shook and the mountain smoked and in awesome solemnity a nation was forged there amongst the jagged fastnesses of coppered Sinai.

Next morning, as the bell of the monastery pealed out its morning call as it has for centuries: 33 strokes, one for each year of Jesus' earthly life. I reflected: Sinai has yielded many treasures: malachite, turquoise and other minerals; icons, mosaics and rare manuscripts; but the greatest treasure bequeathed to mankind from this isolated corner of the Middle East is the Decalogue.

Without a doubt, a momentous event lies behind the survival of the remarkably resilient Jewish race. Throughout millennia the Torah has been its guide, and Hebrew faith was established upon the unshakeable conviction that Moses spoke with God face to face at Horeb. The Ten Commandments have shaped Jewish behavior and molded its conduct, but is such a code given long ages ago to ancient Israel relevant for mankind throughout the ages?

A wealth of newly-unearthed data that illuminates the Bible sheds light also on two of the commandments—the second and the tenth—as we shall soon note. Moreover, the text of the Decalogue as a whole takes on new meaning as we restudy it with the tools and materials of modern scholarship.

The Ten Commandments were originally addressed to the children of Israel. The opening words—*"I am Jehovah, your God, Who brought you from the land of Egypt, from the house of slaves"*—are directed by God to His particular people; but the text is a guide to a way of life worthy of His followers in all ages.

The Commandments are not law in the legal sense. They are beyond law-court legality. We are to obey them, not because there is a penalty for coveting; violating the tenth commandment draws no punishment according to the Bible or to any other code. The Ten Commandments do not even allude to any legal punishment for theft, adultery, or murder. The text enjoins obedience on us for the love of God, not for fear of penalty imposed by a court. It states that while God punishes sins down to the third and fourth generations, he metes out loving-kindness down to thousands of generations *"for those that love Me and keep My commandments."* The commandments are thus beyond law in the ordinary sense, and will be practiced by those who love God, because to love God requires the fulfillment of His commandments. The Hebrews did not have to justify the validity of the commandments, as the Greek philosophers had to justify morality and ethics, for reasons to be given below.

"THOU SHALT HAVE NO OTHER GODS BEFORE ME."

The first commandment forbids the worship of other gods. Israel had been rescued from slavery by its God, who therefore claims Israel's sole allegiance. The chief concern of Israel was with living by the rules of conduct required of them by their God.

The power of the first commandment is borne out by the fact that Israel -with its stubbornly exclusive cult of the one unseen God, ratified among smoke and fire—for well over a thousand years—though pock-marked with lapses into idolatry -stood forth as a lone fortress of monotheism in a pagan world. (*"The Jews,"* marvels the Roman historian Tacitus, *"recognize one sole God, and they perceive Him only with their minds!"*) In return for His abiding presence, the Lord asked for total dedication—or as Martin Luther put it, *"Man's whole heart, along with all his confidence, in God alone and no one else."*

"THOU SHALT NOT MAKE UNTO THEE ANY GRAVEN IMAGE, OR ANY LIKENESS OF ANYTHING THAT IS IN HEAVEN ABOVE, OR THAT IS IN THE EARTH BENEATH, OR THAT IS IN THE WATER UNDER THE EARTH..."

Echoes of old taboos reverberate in this commandment. Primitive people to this day tend to link names with magic—pronouncing someone's name, it is felt, confers control over him. The same applies to the possession of a person's "image," from clay figure to modern photograph. Hence, refrain! God must be sovereign and free—no magic may encroach. His name must not be named outside the act of worship; His effigy must not be made or "bowed to."

As Israel evolved toward a more complex civilization, the minor rule against likenesses of "things"—perhaps in imitation of the Lord's creation—fell by the wayside. The very Temple in Jerusalem, we know, was decorated with carved lions, palm trees, flowers; but over the centuries, not one of the countless spadefuls of Palestinian earth turned over by eager archaeologists has ever given up an image of the Lord, except perhaps that famous picture from Sinai's *Kuntillet Ajrud* from the 9th century BC. Scholars continue to cavil over its meaning—is it a picture of YHWH?

Individual Israelites, however, were not above manufacturing their own private gods. Judges 17 relates how a Hebrew named Michah made an idol of silver and proceeded to set up a private family cult around it. To be sure, this was well meant and all in Jehovah's name; but the fact remains that we have taken an overt step toward breaking with our fathers' faith when we manufacture a new idol and build up our own private cult about it.

The commandments seek to keep the people united by an individual allegiance to God and His rules of living. Making new gods is a sure way of splitting up a community and of breaking up families as well.

What we have just said about the second commandment may seem somewhat farfetched if we try to comprehend the biblical text without some external information. After all, the Ten Commandments were worded directly not for us but for the Near Eastern people over 3,000 years ago. In our quest for a deeper understanding of the Bible, it is always helpful to gain access to pertinent data from biblical antiquity. The second commandment is now

An Adventure into Discovery

illuminated by a legal document from about 1400 B.C. The document is written in Babylonian on a clay tablet and comes from the town of Nuzu located near the modern Iraqi city of Kirkuk. It is the last will and testament of a father to his sons. The father commands his sons not to make other gods. Instead he deposits the household idols with his eldest son so that all his sons will be united through the worship of the family gods at the home of the chief heir:

> "After I die, my sons shall not make gods; my gods I leave with my eldest son."

The religion of that Nuzu man is not like the religion of Moses. (But it is not unlike the religion of Laban, who had such gods, according to Genesis 31.) The Ten Commandments enjoin upon us the worship of one God; and even He must not be represented iconically. The Nuzu family tablet shows us a danger that was recognized in the Bible world; namely, that making idols is divisive and should therefore be shunned. (We cannot enter into all the implications of idolatry in later times, but it is worth noting that defeated nations, on seeing their idols dragged off or smashed, tended to become demoralized and lose their identity. Assyria, Babylonia, the Seleucids, and Rome could not destroy the Jewish religion partly because God and His people's allegiance to Him were incorporeal and therefore indestructible. The second commandment thus paved the way for the historic survival of Judaism). Some of the prophets and the New Testament eschatology envisage the unity of all the nations in peace and in worship, but the Chosen People in the second millennium B.C. did not start out with any ecumenical program for immediate implementation. The structure of society in the Pentateuch is geared to the requirements of a city-state. Pentateuchal regulations are not designed for a country the size of the United States of America, with its great distances and with a population much too large to assemble in the capital.

Encounter at Sinai

The city-state aspect of ancient Israel is not, of course, what made Israel distinctive or great. Other city-states (including Athens and Sparta) also shared the same general structure. What made Israel different and significant was the content of its law that took it out of the religious and moral pattern of all its neighbors. The other nations not only were idolatrous and polytheistic, but also made a place for lax morality and warped ethics. Israel accepted the law that consciously forbade those internationally accepted usages. Nowadays, when biblical teachings are in theory approved (no matter how much they are violated in practice), the Ten Commandments seem self-evident, and it takes less courage to live by them than to flout them; but this was not so for the early Israelites, whose law put them out of step with the world and made them the objects of scorn and hate in pagan antiquity. The Roman historian Tacitus accused the Jews of turning the standards of the world topsy-turvy by inverting the definitions of "sacred" and "impious." From the standpoint of Mediterranean paganism, Tacitus was not entirely wrong. The Pentateuch (e.g. Leviticus 18:1-5, 30) tells us not to follow the customs of other nations, because those customs are abominable; but instead to follow God's laws, which, as we now know, are often in conscious opposition to the laws of Israel's neighbors.

"THOU SHALT NOT TAKE THE NAME OF THE LORD THY GOD IN VAIN..."

The third commandment forbids perjury. It is not an innovation. It was a widespread view that swearing to a falsehood would incite the god invoked to punish the perjurer. The idea is that when we offend God by misusing His name, he avenges His honor by bringing retribution on us.

"REMEMBER THE SABBATH DAY, TO KEEP IT HOLY. SIX DAYS YOU SHALL LABOR AND DO ALL THY WORK BUT THE SEVENTH DAY IS A SABBATH UNTO JEHOVAH YOUR GOD..."

Other nations divided time into units of seven, but it remained for the Bible to establish the seventh-day as a day of rest for the entire community. In the Exodus version, keeping the Sabbath is required by divine example. He labored for six days and rested on the seventh and we should do likewise. The Deuteronomy version, however, stresses the social side. The Israelite was to give his dependents a day of rest for humanitarian reasons (Deuteronomy 5). Israel's slavery had conditioned the nation to understand this commandment.

In antiquity slavery existed everywhere, even in Israel. The abolition of slavery lay ahead in history; but humane treatment of the slave is a divine commandment, and his right to a weekly day of rest is guaranteed by the law. Tyranny can be exercised not only over one's slaves but also over one's children, so the commandment protects them, too. It remains to note that the ancient concept of the community embraces domestic animals as well as people. Accordingly, the work animals are to have their day of rest. It is interesting to note that after the Flood, God made His covenant not only with Noah and his sons but also with the animals on the ark (Genesis 9:8-17). To cite only one of the many more examples: the slaying of the Egyptian firstborn applied to Egyptian cattle as well as people (Exodus 11:5).

"*HONOR THY FATHER AND THY MOTHER: THAT THY DAYS MAY BE LONG UPON THE LAND WHICH THE LORD THY GOD GIVETH THEE.*"

This commandment is the key to social stability. Without it we run into juvenile delinquency and a general breakdown of law and order. Respect for society must be rooted in respect for parents in the home from early childhood. Israel took this responsibility seriously; Deuteronomy 21:18-21 prescribes the death penalty for incorrigible juvenile delinquents for the express purpose of "wiping out evil from the midst" of the community. We do not know how often—or indeed if ever—this drastic measure was implemented; but we do know that ancient

Hebrew society did not spawn whole generations of children who wantonly violated the law and brought disgrace on their parents. No biblical Israelite youth was so rebellious as to come home and slay his parents because they were exercising their parental authority over him and not permitting him to run his life as he pleased. There is no dearth of crime narrated in the pages of Scripture, but the people who considered respect for parents a divine ordinance did not have a problem with juvenile delinquency.

The reward for obedience is long life in the Promised Land. The world as a whole was not yet ready for the Ten Commandments. Many ancient city-states had their own special law codes, but Israel alone had a law that has remained a living force throughout the centuries. Indeed, with the spread of Christianity, it is still widening its influence, whereas the laws of the other ancient nations are objects of study but not guides for living.

It should be noted thus far that the Decalogue prior to this commandment dealt with man's relationship with God. Now it turns to man-to-man relationships. And the fifth commandment forms a bridge, for as we honor our parents, we also honor the Eternal Father in their persons.

"THOU SHALT NOT KILL."

The sixth commandment is not directed against killing in general. Hebrew, like English, has entirely different words for "murder" and "kill." This commandment does not apply, for example, to capital punishment meted out to criminals under law; nor does it apply to killing the enemy on the battlefield. Murder designates assassination or some other kind of treacherous or criminal manslaughter.

One might think that the prohibitions against murder, adultery (the seventh commandment), and stealing (the eighth) would be universal, but it is not so. In ancient Sparta, it was getting caught, not stealing, that was reprehensible. In Canaan the natives worshiped the goddess Anath, who, as we know from the *Ugaritic* poems, had a man murdered to rob him of his bow. (Ugarit was a city-state on the northern coast of Syria. The religious texts found there constituted "the Bible of the Canaanites," so to speak, around 1400-1200 B.C.) The *Homeric Hymn* to Hermes glories in telling how that beloved god was a remarkable thief from infancy, and Zeus himself became enamored of married women—like Amphitryon's wife Alcmene—and impregnated them.

In other words, the Hebrews lived in a world where people revered gods who committed theft, adultery, and murder. In Israel, however, the concept of God left no place for such behavior. Pagan gods—as we know from the religious texts of the pagans themselves—all too often set a sub-human standard for their devotees. In Israel the divine pattern uplifted man. This is why the biblical tradition—in which men are created in the image of God—leads men toward moral perfection by inspiring them to imitate their Maker. We are told, for instance, to follow God's example by resting on the Sabbath. The perfect example of our righteous and unsinning God made it unnecessary for Hebrew moralists to set up a philosophical system for the good way of life. In Israel, right living consisted in conforming to the divine pattern. Conduct was to be in accord with God's commandments.

Another talented people, the Greeks, also aspired to the good life; but they could not do so by emulating their deities. Instead, the Greeks had to justify morality and ethics by systematic philosophy, a development the ancient Hebrews did not experience because they had no need for it. Jehovah provides a pattern for the moral man; Zeus does not.

"THOU SHALT NOT BEAR FALSE WITNESS AGAINST THY NEIGHBOR."

As we shall presently observe, distinguished neighbors of the Hebrews stooped to this crime even though universal agreement held it to be wrong. In Israel, however, it could not go unpunished.

"THOU SHALT NOT COVET THY NEIGHBOR'S HOUSE, THOU SHALT NOT COVET THY NEIGHBOR'S WIFE, NOT HIS MANSERVANT, NOT HIS MAIDSERVANT, NOR HIS OX, NOR HIS ASS, NOR ANYTHING THAT IS THY NEIGHBOR'S."

The tenth commandment often seems enigmatic. Now, can anyone be found guilty of coveting unless it leads to theft or adultery?—and the latter offenses are punishable as such, regardless of the coveting that led to them. In our society, we expect a degree of coveting on the part of any normal person who wants to get ahead. In fact, a young person who does not aspire to get ahead is considered ambitionless. In any case it seems at first strange that the Ten Commandments prohibit coveting, classifying it with theft, adultery, and murder.

The biblical emphasis against coveting is clarified by Ugaritic literature, according to which the pagan god Baal is a god who covets the houses of his fellow gods, and then succeeds in getting the best of all houses built for himself. The Bible is to a great extent a reaction against pagan values. Anything honored in pagan religion is likely to be regarded as an abomination in Israel. It is no accident that the very first article we are told not to covet is our neighbor's house, for Baal coveted just that. Ugaritic literature also tells us that Baal coveted some mythological animals: this is countered by the biblical prohibition against coveting our neighbor's livestock. The version in Deuteronomy 5 adds the field of our neighbor among the objects we must not covet; we may compare the Ugaritic tablet that tells of Baal's coveting fields. The emphasis against coveting is now clear from the Ugaritic texts that attribute covetousness to Baal.

The clash between Israelite and local pagan values is illustrated by the ill-starred marriage of Ahab and Jezebel. Ahab was weak vis-à-vis his foreign wife. Each was a product of his own culture. When Ahab wanted Naboth's vineyard and Naboth refused to sell or trade it, Ahab, though distressed, would not put pressure on Naboth (1 Kings 21).

Ahab as a Hebrew was not to covet another's field, let alone bear false witness, steal, and murder to gain possession of it. Jezebel approached matters differently. She was of Phoenician-Canaanite background and a devotee of Baal. Far from outlawing covetousness, Baal had set the pattern for it. As a result, Jezebel could not understand her husband's scruples, and like her god, she proceeded to get the coveted object. She filched the vineyard for Ahab by trumping up a false accusation against Naboth, hiring lying witnesses against him, and having him murdered so that Ahab could confiscate his property. Nowhere could we find a clearer contrast between Israel and the culture that surrounded it. By her native Phoenician standards, she was a normal queen who never did anything worse than Baal or Anath. Ahab's scruples were as incomprehensible to Jezebel as her behavior is to the average Bible reader today.

Once we grasp the values of Canaanite Baalism, we can begin to understand the magnitude and nature of the reaction embodied in Israel's Yahwism.

Coveting is all too common. It characterizes vulgar people, and while not punishable offense in itself, it frequently is the prelude to open transgression. The tenth commandment is designed to save us from the dangerous blight of such commonness.

The Ten Commandments are a landmark in human history, because they sum up in a few verses so much of what society and the individual need for a good, orderly, and productive life.

The Decalogue consists largely of prohibitions—a dirty word in an anti-authoritarian climate, but nevertheless an important one. "To learn the don'ts in any pursuit, intellectual, in oral or practical is the beginning of wisdom."[30] Actually, the giving of negative commands leaves open more room for freedom of behavior. Compare for example, *"Thou shalt wear blue jeans"* with *"Thou shalt not wear blue jeans."* The positive wording rules out all options but one, whereas the negative wording rules out only one option, leaving others. A list of ten positive commands would have been extremely restrictive, and we'd be wrestling with it to this day.

Modern man has difficulty accepting the "don'ts" of the Decalogue. "Why can't we work out our own code of morality?" he asks. Once the traditional absolutes are relinquished, however, moral relativism results. Like the Greeks of old, man must construct his own system of right and wrong. The end of any such inquiries (if they are successful) must quite closely approximate the Ten Commandments. Men have broken them, ridiculed them, ignored and forgotten them, but never bettered them.

Consider the logical arrangement of the commandments. The first one tells us whom to worship and emphasizes the exclusiveness of divine worship. The second one tells us how to worship, setting forth a standard of spirituality for all religious activities. The commandment concerning reverence suggests the approach for worship. All that is needed now is a time for worship, and the Sabbath commandment provides this.

The fourth commandment having already mentioned the family, the fifth refers to that authority which stands next to God, namely that of parents. In the family, life begins; therefore the sixth commandment deals with life and its preservation: "Thou shalt not kill."

Because life comes in two forms, male and female, the seventh commandment regulates the relationship between the sexes: "Thou shalt not commit adultery." In the family not only life and the sexes have their origin, but also property. Thus the eighth commandment safeguards possessions: "Thou shalt not steal." Something else that must be safeguarded besides life, purity, and property is reputation, and the ninth commandment rears a protecting hedge for that also. "Thou shalt not bear false witness against thy neighbor."

The final commandment goes to the root of sin. It deals with our thinking. We are not even to think wrongly. "Thou shalt not covet." In the New Testament, covetousness is described as "idolatry" (Colossians 3:5), and thus the tenth commandment is linked with the first two. The Ten Commandments constitute a great circle without beginning or end, for a circle is the symbol of perfection and eternity. What a changed world this would be were all men to walk according to this law of love!

Consider also the principles embodied in the Ten Commandments. The principle of the first commandment is loyalty; of the second, worship; and then, in order, come reverence, sanctification, respect for authority, love, purity, honesty, truthfulness, and contentment. These are not only the principles that represent God's ideal of character, but they are also the laws of life and can never become out of date.

We have too often failed to realize that when God gave this law, He was in love with mankind, telling them how to live in order to get the most unadulterated happiness from life (Deuteronomy 33:1-3; 10:13). At Sinai, then He revealed the great secrets of the universe, particularly these three: (1) that life is dependent upon law, and that happiness is dependent upon obedience; (2) that we need a hierarchy of values, with God at the top of the hierarchy; and (3) that people are more important than things. The order of the Ten Commandments is God, people, things. Sadness and loss come if we reverse the order, putting things first and God last. (Matthew 6:33; Luke 12:15-31)

God greatly honored this law. Palestine of old was the center of the world (Ezekiel 5:5), but the center of Palestine was its capital, Jerusalem. At the center of Jerusalem was the Temple, and in the center of the Temple was the most holy place. In the center of the most holy place rested the Ark of the Covenant, which enshrined the law of God. God made it central in the world because He wished us to make it central in our lives. It is to our advantage if we do.

> "If only you had listened to God's commands your prosperity would have been on like a river in flood and your just success like the waves of the sea."—Isaiah 48:18.

IX
A STATUE FOR REMEMBRANCE

"This is my Father's world, and to my listening ears,
  All nature sings, and round me rings
  The music of the spheres.
This is my Father's world, I rest me in the thought
  Of rocks and trees, of skies and seas
  His hand the wonders wrought."
    —Maltbie D. Babcock

If we had lived in the third century B. C. and sailed into Rhodes harbor at sunrise, we would have seen something which had never existed before and has never existed since: a bronze statue, more than twenty times the height of a man, up reared against the sky, and shining in the dawn light; the figure of a god in the image of a man, so huge, and yet so exquisitely proportioned, as to overwhelm all by its beauty. Shakespeare described this ancient wonder when he put these words into the mouth of Cassius in *Julius Caesar*:

  "...he doth bestride the narrow world
  Like a Colossus; and we petty men
  Walk under his huge legs, and peep about
  To find ourselves dishonorable graves."

These lines embody a medieval tradition concerning the Colossus of Rhodes; a tradition that the Colossus actually bestrode the harbor entrance, one foot on each arm of the jetty. If any of us still cling to this illusion, we had better forget it at once, for no ancient writer who saw the statue suggests that it was so large, or that it straddled the harbor entrance. Huge it certainly was. Pliny wrote of it:

"Most worthy of admiration is the colossal statue of the sun which stood formerly at Rhodes, and was the work of Chares the Lindian, no less than seventy cubits in height. The statue, fifty-six years after it was erected, was thrown down by an earthquake, yet even as it lies

An Adventure into Discovery

it excites our wonder and imagination. Few men can clasp the thumb with their arms, and the fingers are larger than most statues. When the limbs are broken asunder, vast caverns are seen yawning in the interior. Within, too, are to be seen large masses of rocks, by the aid of which the artist steadied it while erecting it."

Philon of Byzantium, when in about 146 B.C. he wrote the first book on the *Seven Wonders of the World*, described the statue as follows:

The Colossus of Rhodes

"At Rhodes was set up a Colossus 70 cubits high, representing the Sun; for the similitude of the God was known only to his descendants. The artist expended as much bronze on it as seemed likely to create a dearth at the foundries; for the casting of the statue was the world's (triumph) in metal working...The artist fortified the bronze from within by means of iron scaffolding and squared blocks of stone, whose connecting rods bear witness to hammering of Cyclopean force, and indeed the hidden part of the labor is greater than the visible...He constructed beneath it a base of white marble, and on this, working out the proportion, he first fixed the feet of the Colossus up as far as the ankle bones, on which the god, 70 cubits high, was to be erected."

Philon then describes how Chares, having first made a model of the statue,

"...cast the parts separately in bronze, and, as each was fitted into position, the next part above it was cast and fitted, and so on until the Colossus was completed. The sculptor (he concludes) then continually piled up around the yet uncompleted parts of the Colossus a vast mound of earth, which had the completed parts and allowed the casting of the next stages at ground level. So, going up bit by bit towards the goal of his endeavor, at the expense of 500 talents of bronze and 300 of iron, he made his god equal to the God, raising a work mighty in its boldness; for he gave to the world a second Sun to match the first."[31]

Philon was a mechanician, and therefore greatly interested in the technical construction of the statue, but perhaps even more remarkable is the fact that it was also a great work of art. Those who saw it—men who had as standards of comparison the works of Pheidias and Praxiteles—have stated that it was not merely the largest but was also the most perfect model of a human form ever fashioned by man; and yet there is a story—we do not know if true—that the sculptor, having nearly completed his work, discovered he had made an error in his calculations, and committed suicide.

From the description of Philon, Pliny and others, it is quite clear that the Colossus was a nude figure of the sun-god Helios (Apollo), standing with feet together on a high plinth, built at the end of a mole or jetty over-looking the harbor. Its height, according to a critical study made by Herbert Maryon, was about 120 feet from head to feet, apart from the plinth on which it stood, which was as Philon says, itself higher than most statues. From ground level, therefore, the Colossus probably rose to a height of 150 feet, half the height of New York's Statue of Liberty. It was built of enormous plates of bronze, though these, according to Maryon's calculations, were only about the thickness of a penny. It was for this reason that the statue was strengthened internally by massive iron stanchions reinforced by blocks of stone.

How certain can we be that the descriptions of Philon are true? There is a sculptured relief found in Rhodes only a few years ago which, although it cannot be precisely dated, seems to depict the Colossus; the style is in keeping and the stance of the statue is appropriate to the subject. It shows a nude man, with drapery slung over his left arm, shading his eyes with his right hand as if gazing at some distant object. The relief is badly damaged and only the upper part survives, but a third-century coin with the head of Helios shows the god's face surrounded by spiked "rays." This, probably, is how Chares adorned the head of his Colossus.

Why was the Colossus built? The answer to that question provides a story of heroism almost as exciting as the building of the statue itself. Rhodes, a small island off the southwest coast of Asia Minor, was always of great strategic and commercial importance. As far back as Mycenaean times (ca. 1500 B.C.), its people were notable seafarers and traders; they had contracts with the island civilization of Crete, and later, when the Dorian Greeks colonized Rhodes, in about 1000 B.C., they built at its north-eastern end a harbor and a city which rivaled Athens. As metalworkers, the Rhodians were famous from the Nile to the Euphrates, and in time grew so wealthy that they aroused the jealousy of the Athenians, to whom, in the end, they had to concede supremacy. Nevertheless their sea-borne trade continued to flourish, and their prosperity increased. For a time they came under the dominion of Mausolus, the Carian king from Asia Minor, whose tomb later became another of the Seven Wonders; then, in the fifth century, Rhodes fell to the Persian conqueror Darius, who absorbed it into his empire.

In 340 B.C. Alexander the Great delivered the island, but, though a Macedonian, he was a Hellene like the Rhodians themselves, and the yoke he imposed on them was light. On Alexander's death, they became free again, and then began their period of great power and prosperity. When the new capital, Alexandria, became the chief center of Mediterranean trade, the Rhodian ships carried to it the riches of the East, and distributed the products of Egypt all over the Mediterranean world. It was this close association with the Ptolemaic capital that led the islanders into war. When Ptolemy I was engaged in war with Antigonus, ruler of Macedon, the Rhodians supported him with their ships. Antigonus did not forget this and,

A Statue for Remembrance

in 307 B.C. sent a strong punitive expedition to Rhodes commanded by his son, Demetrius. Forty thousand men sailed with Demetrius—more than the entire population of Rhodes—and in addition he carried with him the most powerful siege-artillery of his time, battering rams, spring guns and the like.

It seemed impossible that the little island would withstand such an armada. But the Rhodians, undeterred, made their preparations. Historians tell us that slaves were given arms, and promised their freedom if Demetrius was defeated. Women gave their hair to make bowstrings, and worked through the night making ammunitions. Where the walls needed strengthening, the Rhodians pulled down their temples and used the stones to consolidate their defenses. Beleaguered, isolated, without hope of help, they fought on, while Demetrius and his forty thousand delivered attack after attack, battering their way nearer and nearer to the citadel. Invitations to surrender were contemptuously flung back. Starvation and disease could not weaken resistance. The Rhodians, after all, were Greeks, and they had before them the examples of Marathon and Thermopylae. Like the Spartans of Thermopylae, they fought with determination and without hope. But unlike the Spartans, who died almost to the last man, the courage of the Rhodians was rewarded.

In 306 B.C., Ptolemy, remembering the services the islanders had given him, arrived off the island with a powerful fleet. Demetrius was forced to withdraw, and Rhodes was saved.

As a gesture of gratitude to Ptolemy, to whom they gave the name Soter (Savior), by which he is still known, the islanders resolved to erect a monument which would perpetuate the memory of their deliverance; but—and here is the difference between our world and that of the ancients—they did not erect a statue to Ptolemy, as the British placed a statue of Franklin Roosevelt in Grosvenor Square, London. Instead, they commissioned Chares, the pupil of the renowned Lysippus, favorite of Alexander, to make an enormous statue of their protecting deity, the sun-god Helios, and erect it at the entrance to their harbor. And this statue for remembrance was built from the materials of the abandoned siege-machines of the defeated Demetrius. The engines were melted down to provide bronze, and Chares began his great work.

Another statue for remembrance was set in history; not a statue that could be demolished by an earthquake as was the Colossus of Rhodes in 224 B.C. and 443 years later be sold as scrap metal, a miserable heap of 300 tons of bronze carted away on the back of 900 camels! Rather, a particular twenty-four hour period, a day that would memorialize the birthday of the world fifty-two times every year as long as earth remains. This memorial is identified in the creation epic recorded in the book of Genesis.

> "Thus the heavens and the earth were finished, and all the host of them. And on the seventh day God ended his work which he had made; and he rested on the seventh day from all his work which he had made. And God blessed the seventh day, and sanctified it: because that in it he had rested from all—his work which God created and made." —Genesis 2:1-3

The perpetuity of the Sabbath as a day to "remember" creation was concretized by its inclusion in the ten commandments several thousand years later, "for in six days the Lord made heaven and earth, the sea, and all that in them is, and rested the seventh day: wherefore the Lord blessed the sabbath day, and hallowed it."—Exodus 20:11.

John Milton, author of *Paradise Lost*, said: "The reason for which the commandment itself was originally given, namely as a memorial of God's having rested from the creation of the world...." And later, John Wesley commented: "The Sabbath is the memorial of the creation, the sign of God's creative power, God designed that through keeping it man should forever remember Him as the true and living God, the Creator of all things."

A Statue for Remembrance

Interestingly, there is no certain evidence of a seventh-day Sabbath in any ancient nation but Israel. Neither Assyria, nor Babylon, nor any other nation knew of a seventh-day Sabbath quite like Israel's. Only the people of Israel, later known as the Jews, celebrated a Sabbath-day rest every week. We are obligated then to ask the Jews for the origin and meaning of the Sabbath. They testify unanimously that the seventh day Sabbath, together with the week, was instituted at the very beginning of the human race, by its Maker, as a divine gift that heaven and earth might be united in an everlasting covenant.

All primary human questionings find their answer in the Sabbath. The late philosopher Edward G. Spaulding said there are only three main questions that every age must ask:

(1) "From what source do we come?"
(2) "Toward what goal do we rightly move?"
(3) "Why?"

The Sabbath answers all three. It declares:

(1) That we come from a loving Heavenly Father who wishes to share His joy,
(2) That ultimately our world will become like the sinless Eden which the holy memorial commemorates, and
(3) That the reason for our existence is that we might become like our Maker in righteous character, even as it was a man in the image of God who first enjoyed Sabbath communion with Him.

Two thousand years ago Jesus proclaimed that "The Sabbath was made for man" (*Mark* 2:27). The Sabbath then, is here for humanity. It is to minister to our humanness. One writer suggests, "The value of the Sabbath as a means of education is beyond estimate. Whatever of ours God claims from us He returns again enriched, transfigured with His own glory".[32] The Sabbath, then, is to help man become all he can be in the presence of God by the grace of God.

An Adventure into Discovery

How well adapted then, is this benevolent gift of a holy day? Its chief importance is not that it meets man's physical needs for rest, but that it meets his needs as a spiritual creature. When the Romans met the Jews and noticed their strict adherence to the law of abstaining from labor on the Sabbath, their only reaction was contempt. The Sabbath is a sign of Jewish indolence, was the opinion held by Juvenal, Seneca and others.

In defense of the Sabbath, Philo, the spokesman of the Greek-speaking Jews of Alexandria, says:

> "On this day we are commanded to abstain from all work, not because the law inculcates slackness...Its object is rather to give man relaxation from continuous and unending toil and by refreshing their bodies with a regularly calculated system of remissions to send them out renewed to their old activities. For a breathing spell enables not merely ordinary people but athletes also to collect their strength with a stronger force behind them to undertake promptly and patiently each of the tasks set before them."[33]

Here the Sabbath is represented not in the spirit in which it was given but in the spirit of Aristotle. According to the Stagirite, "we need relaxation, because we cannot work continuously. Relaxation, then, is not an end"; it is "for the sake of activity," for the sake of gaining strength for new efforts.[34] To the Jewish mind, however, labor is the means toward an end, and the Sabbath as a day of rest, as a day of abstaining from toil, is not for the purpose of recovering one's lost strength and becoming fit for the forthcoming labor. The Sabbath is a day for the sake of life. Man is not a beast of burden, and the Sabbath is not for the purpose of enhancing the efficiency of his work. "Last in creation, first in intention," the Sabbath is "the end of the creation of the heaven and earth."[35]

Thus the Sabbath is not for the sake of the weekdays; the weekdays are for the sake of the Sabbath. It is not an interlude but the climax of living. A busy editorial writer, whose eyes began to trouble her, was obliged to visit a specialist. She told him she thought she needed a new pair of glasses, but the specialist replied that her real need was not for new spectacles but rest for the eyes. The woman responded that such was impossible, for her work compelled her to sit all day bending over a desk reading and writing. Upon inquiring where she lived and finding that it was in full sight of the Blue Ridge Mountains in the Alleghenies, the specialist advised her,

> "Go home and do your work as usual, but every hour or so leave your desk and go stand on your porch and look at the mountains. The far-away look will rest your eyes after the long strain of reading manuscripts and proof sheets."

This is exactly what Sabbaths are for—they are the faraway looks that rest, sustain, and inspire the soul; they represent a liberation from routine to enable us to reorient our lives to our ultimate commitment.

D. M. Canright once wrote:

> "Deprive society wholly of this weekly rest-day; abolish your Sabbath schools, prayer meetings, and regular sermons; let work of all kinds and classes go on seven days in the week, and what would society be? If you want to know, go to heathen lands where they have entirely forgotten the Sabbath, and behold their ignorance, superstition, degradation, and crime. That is just what would follow, in any nation, the abolition of the weekly rest-day."[36]

The Sabbath, by putting all things in true perspective, meets that need of the soul to worship and adore the highest good. Worship comes from "worth-ship". The distinction between Creator and creature is marked out by creation's memorial, and weekly the reminder is afforded that one of the things made are adequate to satisfy the human spirit, and therefore they should never receive first place in the soul's adoration.

It is as though God had said to Adam after his creation on the sixth day, "*Adam, behold this wonderful world—full of objects animated and inanimate which call for admiration; but beware—none of them, nor all of them, can satisfy you, not even Eve. You were made for Me, your heart can find rest only in Me, its source; therefore let us spend your first whole day together as a pattern for your life hereafter."* At that juncture God ushered in sacred time with the glory of the first sunset Adam had ever seen (Leviticus 23:32). What a wonderfully exciting time that first whole day of existence must have been for Adam and Eve! They walked and talked with their Maker and found in Him their fountain of joy and their source of truth and strength. That first Sabbath was God's acted-out invitation to all men to find their rest in him.

The Colossus of Rhodes was built as a monument to a remarkable deliverance. At the time of Israel's liberation from Egyptian bondage the Sabbath acquired another meaning. Sabbath rest was enjoined as a memorial of God's mighty deliverance of His people. After the reiteration of the Sabbath commandment recorded in Deuteronomy 5:15, God said:

> "You shall remember that you were a servant in the land of Egypt, and the Lord your God brought you out thence with a mighty hand and with outstretched arm; therefore, the Lord your God commanded you to keep the Sabbath day."

It is worth noticing that while in Genesis 2:2 and Exodus 20:8-11 the Sabbath rest is founded on the completion of God's work of Creation, in Deuteronomy 5:12-15 the Sabbath rest is presented as the memorial of another significant act of God, that is, His extraordinary deliverance of the people from the Egyptian bondage. To the original motif of the completion of Creation is now added the Sabbath rest, in the light of the Exodus experience, the significance of deliverance and freedom.

The Israelite, who had known oppression, poverty, pain, and slavery in Egypt and who had been delivered by God's mighty hand, was now invited by God to commemorate that divine deliverance, not only by resting himself but by making it possible for all his dependents, even the animals, to enjoy a full day of rest. It is quite remarkable when it is noted that through the Sabbath rest, the Israelite re-enacted God's marvelous original deliverance. Every seven days, seven years, and seven weeks of years, the Israelite entered into a renewed experience of liberation, both by resting himself and by rendering free all men, beasts and property. At the setting of the sun all men were to become free and equal before God. The uneven divisions of the Hebrew society were leveled out as the Sabbath began. Servants, as well as masters were to rest. The Sabbath was the great equalizer.

It was God's plan that the weekly Sabbath rest, if properly observed, would have constantly delivered man from the bondage of the type that Egypt represented, which is not limited to any country or century, but which includes every land and every age. Man needs today to be delivered from the bondage that comes from the greediness for always greater gains and power; the bondage of social inequalities of rich and poor, high and low, of the "haves" and "have-nots"; the bondage of sin and selfishness. The Sabbath rest was divinely designed to deliver man weekly from his measureless selfishness and lead him back to God.

P. Massi pointedly observes that "a break from work is necessary to the modern man, victim of sin, in order to offer a barrier against that exaggerated selfish tendency, which makes of our I the center and measure of all, so that we may be brought to recognize God as the owner of the universe and that we may engage ourselves in leading back all things to God."[37]

The New Testament indicates that the Sabbath is a memorial not only of creation but also of redemption. Jesus on the sixth day of His last week of redemption cried, "It is finished," and then rested. He could have risen the next day, but He chose to rest in death that Sabbath, as He had rested each Sabbath of His life. Henceforth, every

Sabbath would be a reminder of the finished work of redemption—a memorial of the Creator's love manifested in the re-creation of redemption. The Sabbath thus becomes an emblem of our peace in Christ through His completed work of atonement, a seal of righteousness by faith, for the essence of faith in the looking away to Another in acknowledgement of one's creaturely dependence.

The Sabbath rest as a medium of man's deliverance from sin is portrayed in the example and teachings of Jesus. Jesus proclaims Himself the Lord of the Sabbath in order to demonstrate that He has the authority to determine in what manner the Sabbath is to be kept so that God is honored. As Lord of the Sabbath He enunciated the principle that "it is lawful to do good on the Sabbath" (Matthew 12:12, RSV), but also through His forceful example He demonstrated how to relieve the physical and spiritual needs of man on the Sabbath day. Five episodes of healing performed by Christ on the Sabbath are reported by the Gospel writers (Matthew 12:9-21; Mark 3:1-6; Luke 6:6-11; 13:10-17; 14:1-6; John 5:1-16; 9:1-38.) It was Christ's positive example and command "to do good on the Sabbath" that led the Pharisees to take "counsel against him, how to destroy him" (verse 14). Referring to another healing performed by Christ on the Sabbath, John similarly testifies: "Thus was why the Jews persecuted Jesus, because he did this on the Sabbath" (John 5:16, RSV).

The Sabbath rest is presented by Christ in a new perspective that is manifested in the precept of performing humanitarian deeds.

> "As 'Lord of the Sabbath' He is supreme but He puts forth no abrogating power when He stated its purport to be the good of man. 'The Sabbath was made for man.'—Mark 2:27. This is a mighty word. It looks backward—onward. It seems to say, it always has been, for man always had need. It always shall be, for man will always need. Thus Jesus decks the Sabbath with undying freshness."[38]

A Statue for Remembrance

The student of Christ's life will note that the Edenic institutions of the Sabbath and marriage Christ labored untiringly to redeem from human perversion. Thus He condemned Pharisaical Sabbathkeeping and traditions which made light of the family relationships. (See Matthew 12, 15, 19; Mark 2). Our Lord did nothing like this for any of the ceremonial requirements which were soon to vanish away, but He recognized in the Sabbath and marriage the twin legacies of Eden and the foundation of society and morality.

On Sinai the Lawgiver spoke of Himself as Creator and Redeemer, A God Who personified that righteousness which the Ten Commandments describe. He sketched man's nature by revealing him as a dependent creature prone to evil in the various ways elaborated by the respective enactments, yet one who, by divine grace, could come to know the prohibitions as promises of a holy life available to him.

The author on the Sinai Summit

Right in the bosom of that law God placed a unique commandment, one enshrining in symbol and parable the main essentials of knowledge for created beings and commemorating forever the towering pillars of existence, namely creation and redemption. The Sabbath commandment is one which man would never have thought out for himself, a commandment which, if observed would guarantee right behavior by steering aright every choice of life. It is one which answers all of man's primary questions and simultaneously points the way to happiness here and hereafter. No wonder the Scriptures refers to it as holy, blessed, and honorable. And because of its supreme importance, to this section only of the divine code the word "remember" was appended.

An Adventure into Discovery

The Scripture declares that a sanctified life inevitably springs from true Sabbath observance. Ezekiel writes of God's declaration, "I gave them my Sabbaths, to be a sign between me and them, that they might know that I am the Lord that sanctify them."—Ezekiel 20:12. Many theologians have commented upon this relationship. Robert Haldane wrote as follows:

> "The fourth commandment is closely connected with the other commandments; but so far from having any Jewish origin, it is the first and only commandment announced in the opening of the sacred canon, and was imposed on our first parents in their state of uprightness and innocence. It thus stands in a peculiar manner at the head of all the commandments, and involves in its breach the abandonment equally of the first and second tables of the decalogue. It is placed at the end of the first table, as the tenth is at the end of the second, as the safeguard of all the rest. It stands between the two tables of our duty to God and our duty to man, as the great foundation and cornerstone binding both together—its observance supporting and conducing to our obedience to the whole."[39]

It is significant indeed that Christ's last reference to the Sabbath is similar in spirit to the emphasis He had given in Eden and at Sinai regarding remembering that holy institution. In His sermon regarding the fall of Jerusalem and the end of the world, Jesus bade His followers to pray regularly concerning their observance of the Sabbath. "Pray ye that your flight be not in the winter, neither on the Sabbath day," said Jesus. (Matthew 24:20) Winter flight would be arduous for the body, and Sabbath flight would be bitter to the soul, as contrary to the design of that holy day.

In the same sermon Christ says, "And take heed to yourselves, lest at any time your hearts be overcharged with surfeiting, and drunkenness, and cares of this life, and so that day come upon you unawares." (Luke 21:34). These statements are complementary. Christ is warning those who live amid the worldliness of time's last hour that in order to be ready for His appearing, in order to avoid the snare of engrossment with earthly matters, they need regularly to pray that their Sabbath-keeping might be all that God intended it to be.

"The Sabbath was made for man," Jesus declared. Modern man needs the Sabbath. In an industrial society where work makes man a cog in a machine and a number in a computer, man needs the Sabbath rest to retain his individuality; to rediscover His Creator and Redeemer; to remember and alleviate the needs of friends and foes; and to strengthen and deepen those human relationships that are often neglected during the busy working week. The Sabbath rests contains for the Christian today, as well as for the Israelite of old, a message and a promise of God's deliverance and of God's desire for man to be totally free and to find rest in Him. The one who enters into the Sabbath rest, dedicating 24 hours to God, proclaims in a tangible way that God has delivered him from the bondage of sin and has empowered him to extend the same deliverance to his fellow men.

Can we be numbered among His disciples who "remember" Him and His law of love and His holy memorial, or do we, like the Rhodians who failed to re-erect the Colossus which lay on the ground—a fallen giant—for 800 years, forget the One who saved us from death?

"A Sabbath well spent, brings a week of content
And joy for the work of the morrow;
But a Sabbath profaned whate'er may be gained
Is a certain forerunner of sorrow."

X
HOAXED AT THE KRAK DES CHEVALIERS

"In religion,
What damned error, but some sober brow
Will bless it, and approve it with a text,
Hiding the grossness with fair ornament?"[40]

The day was blistering hot; for much more than half an hour, it seemed, our jeep slowed and bumped its way up a rough desert track which wound deeper and deeper into the hills near the Syrian frontier. The road grew steeper; our wheels crunched the loose pebbles, and blown sand stung one's eyes. How much longer, I thought? Then suddenly and without warning, there appeared, on the crest of a range of hills, a sight which brought me to me feet. I clung on to the rim of the windshield to get a better view. I am not sure what I had expected, perhaps a few sand-eroded walls and ruined towers. But this was tremendous; a huge and perfectly preserved twelfth-century castle, the largest I had ever seen. From the highest rank of crenellated towers, from the double concentric row of curtain walls to the mighty barbican, it was complete.

I tried to compare it with castles of Britain and Europe. Kenilworth, Manorbier, Chateau Gaillard? They were mere ruins set among green meadows and pastures, romantic in a Tennysonian way, but dead. Warwick, Arundel, Windsor? They were reasonably complete but had been altered, restored, civilized; had become mere decorative appendages to the towns which they adjoined; in any case one could have put any one of them inside this castle and left room to spare.

Here, I suddenly felt that the Middle Ages had thrust themselves uncompromisingly upon me. How often one has read in travel-books such phrases *"one almost expects to see the armored knights riding out from under the gatehouse and crossing the drawbridge, armor gleaming and pennons flying"*. It is never true; all one "expects to see" are lolly-sucking children, crowds of tourists with cameras, and uninformed guides with prepared patter. But not here. It was indeed as if the Knights Hospitallers were still looking out from these grim battlements towards the Moslem hinterland where their enemies lay.

Nor did this impression fade as we came nearer. The walls and towers soared higher and higher into the hot blue sky; one's eyes took in the great sloping wall called "the Mountain," eighty feet thick at the base, which guards the Inner Ward, the concentric lines of massive curtain-wall, pierced with arrow slits, and broken at intervals by the bulging bastions, some round, some square, which housed the defenders and provided enfilading fire along the walls' length. Still higher ran the battlemented sentry-walk and above that, but higher and set back from the outer wall, rose yet another rampart set with towers, enclosing massive buildings. All was built on solid rock, so that it could not be mined. Here were the Middle Ages with their teeth un-drawn.

The Krak des Chevalier, Syria

We had arrived at the *Krak des Chevaliers* and relived the Crusades. Well, of course one knew about the Crusades...Raymond of Toulouse, Godfrey de Bouillon,

An Adventure into Discovery

Count Baldwin, Richard Coeur de Lion, Saladin; that story of how they tested the sharpness of their swords... Richard cutting through the iron bar; Saladin tossing a silk cushion into the air and slicing it in half...schoolboy stuff; Peter the hermit preaching in the market-squares of France, the Children's Crusade, the sack of Jerusalem, the Norman nobles carving out kingdoms for themselves along the shores of the Levant. An isolated, abortive, and not very glorious episode in the history of Christendom.

We crossed the modern bridge which spans the outer ditch, and passed under the towering gateway. No one stopped us; no one demanded tickets; no flock of visitors meekly waited to be shepherded around the building. Immediately upon entering we began our long climb up a flight of stone steps which led to the inner courts. This stairway, twelve feet wide, the width of an English country-road, was built into the thickness of the wall. It had chambers on the outer side with guardrooms capable of holding hundreds of armed men. At the height of its power the Krak held a garrison of two thousand.

At one point during our climb we stepped aside to enter the high, vaulted Banqueting Hall of the Knights, 120 feet long, and nearby cellars, in which huge wine-jars could still be seen, sunk into the floor. Higher still we came out into an open courtyard between the first and second line of ramparts. Here, if one could shut out the brown, sun-scorched rock of the mountains, one might have been in medieval France. There were graceful Gothic buildings with delicate foliated lancets and coats-of-arms which took one immediately to the chateaux of the Loire. For the first time the far-off Crusades became present reality. Here was medieval Christendom's answer to Abdul Malek's "Dome of the Rock"; a million tons of masonry grasping the alien rock, an architecture born in Ile de France transplanted to the arid hills of Syria; clustered columns and high, arching vaults echoing the cadences of Mass' ruddy-faced men from Gascony, Picardy and Pouraine, sweating under the weight of chain-mail, with the Cross emblazoned on their surcoats.

Hoaxed at the Krak des Chevaliers

In imagination one could see it all: the tired faces of the archers at their stations, staring out through the embrasures at the hot, hostile desert—and hear it too: the clank of steel-shod feet echoing along the vaulted corridors; the babble of medieval French.

Higher still we climbed, up broad stone stairways to the Inner Ward, surrounded by a second line of walls and towers. From this high point the building seemed like a great stone ship forever rising the billowing crests of the hills. A high wind roared and buffeted the towers, and high above us an eagle hung poised, balanced against the gale. To the west I looked across the mountain chain towards the distant Mediterranean. Turning half-around I could see the broad sand-brown valley which led to the Moslem hinterland. The military architect who chose the site knew his business.

Nor was the castle isolated. From its towers it could send fire-signals to other castles at Chastel Blanc, Arima, and Tortosa on the coast. Carrier pigeons were also used for communication, an art which the Crusaders learned from the Saracens. And, I was told, there were many such Crusader fortresses in the Lebanon, strategically sited and garrisoned to enable a relatively small number of men to control an area in which they were vastly outnumbered.

Once this fact is grasped the logic of the Crusader castles becomes obvious; yet how many of us have given it any thought? One was aware that the Crusaders invaded Syria and Palestine, and took Jerusalem. One is less aware that for about 125 years they held and administered a kingdom 450 miles long, comprising the County of Tripoli, the Kingdom of Jerusalem and the Principality of Antioch. It was a long, narrow strip flanked by the sea on the west and the hostile Moslem lands to the east. They did this with a ridiculously small number of men, for although the army which started from Nicaea in 1097 was very large; its losses on the long march were enormous. It is doubtful if there were more than 50,000 men who

An Adventure into Discovery

laid siege to Antioch, and as the army moved nearer and nearer to Jerusalem it lost more and more men, some through disease, some in battle, and many who followed their feudal lords as each appropriated for himself domains in the new territories. Robin Fedden writes:

> "By the time the army reached Jerusalem in 1099 it comprised probably not more than fifteen hundred knights, and ten times as many foot soldiers. After the city had fallen, and the primary object of the Crusade had been attained, many of the Ranks with their followers returned to Europe. Godfrey de Bouillon was left to run a kingdom with about three hundred mounted knights."[41]

Admittedly this was only the Kingdom of Jerusalem, but the rulers of the adjoining domains faced the same problem—how to maintain their hold over their newly won lands with Moslem hordes many times their number continually threatening their eastern flank. The answer is clear when one sees, for the first time, these colossal fortresses, of which the Krak des Chevaliers is only one of many. Leonard Cottrell writes:

> "Some are camped on precipitous ravines, or set on bare desert crests, guarding the passes which pierce the mountain wall; others stare across the empty plain which rolls eastward to the Euphrates. There is nothing like them in the world; in sheer size, strength and lonely splendor they outvie most of the medieval castles of Europe, and their very silence and isolation, lapped around by deserts and mountains, emphasizes their grandeur."[42]

The Christian knights who manned these fortresses were strongly influenced by the Oriental way of life. Apart from the religious differences which divided them, they had much in common with the hereditary caste which ruled Islam; both were members of a feudal aristocracy; both loved war and the chase; both were brave and often chivalrous. When Saladin was besieging Kerak of Moab, another Crusader castle east of the Dead Sea, the Chris-

Hoaxed at the Krak des Chevaliers

tian Governor sent to the Saracen leader a gift of meat and wine, informing him that his daughter was to be married that day. Saladin gracefully acknowledged the gift, and sent a message asking the Governor of the castle kindly to inform him which suite was the bridal suite, so that he could avoid bombarding it. On another occasion the Christian commander of Antioch, Tancred, sent one of the knights to the Saracen Lord of Sheizar with the following letter: *"This is a revered knight of the Franks who has completed his pilgrimage and is now on his way back to his country. He asked me to introduce him to you so that he may see your cavaliers. Accordingly I have sent him to you. Treat him well...."*

Nevertheless, despite these humane interludes, the war continued, year after year, while the Saracens grew stronger and the Crusades' numerical strength dwindled. One by one the castles fell to the Moslems, but the Krak des Chevaliers held out alone when all the surrounding fortresses had been taken. Only three hundred knights manned its defenses, yet, even when the outer wall was breached and they were forced to take refuge in the southern redoubt, they never surrendered. Nor could the Saracen commander, the Sultan Beibars, storm the inner citadel.

In the end the rascal Sultan resorted to a trick, a hoax. He smuggled into the castle a message, purporting to come from the Count of Tripoli, ordering the warden of the castle to lay down his arms and march out under safe conduct, which the enemy had guaranteed. The Warden accepted the message as genuine, and the garrison marched out, unmolested by the Moslem besiegers, down the valley and away to the coast, never to return.

Mass was no longer sung in the chapel high above the southern redoubt. The banqueting hall stood empty, the wine-jars unfilled, and French voices were heard no more in the echoing corridors. The Krak des Chevaliers fell because a false message was believed. The Crusaders left,

An Adventure into Discovery

leaving only a castle as a monument—stranded like the bones of an extinct monster, in the sun-baked Levant.

A hoax is "a made-up-story." Men still believe them and often traditions perpetuate the "made-up-story." Interestingly, some of history's greatest hoaxes have come bearing the name of religion. Truth can be counterfeited. Principles can be misrepresented. Faith can be controverted. Right can be obscured. But time cannot sanction error. Custom cannot give it merit; nor age declare it deserving honor. The dictum of history is that truth has ever suffered from the gradual insidious encroachments of error when time, custom, or tradition, have combined to usurp its authority. James Russell Lowell sensed it when he writes:

> *"Careless seems the Great Avenger;*
> *History's pages but record one death grapple*
> *In the darkness 'twixt old systems and the Word.*
> *Truth for ever on the scaffold,*
> *Wrong for ever on the throne;*
> *Yet the scaffold sways the future,*
> *And behind the dim unknown standeth God within*
>   *the shadow,*
> *Keeping watch above His own."*

The leaders of Judaism severely indicted the conduct of Jesus' disciples for neglecting ceremonial washings before they ate their food. This was in violation of the "tradition" of the elders. Jesus responded by pointing out their own inconsistency when He said: "Why do ye also transgress the commandment of God by your tradition? For God commanded, saying, Honor thy father and mother." Their tradition stated in effect that if a son pledged his money or property, setting it apart for temple treasury, he would have no obligation to his parents, even though they were in want. Jesus charged these leaders with hypocrisy, saying, "Thus have ye made the commandment of God of none effect by your tradition." Further, He said: But in vain they do worship me, teaching for doctrines the commandments of men." (Matthew 15:1-9). Jesus applied this vain worship to the setting aside of the fifth commandment. When informed that these leaders, the Pharisees, had taken offense at His remarks, He replied, "Every plant, which My heavenly Father hath not planted, shall be rooted up." Hence the alteration or substitution of any of the commandments stands equally condemned.

It is apparent that another commandment besides the fifth in the enduring ten has been set aside by custom and tradition. Commenting on the blue laws, under "The Law" section "Blue Sunday," in TIME Magazine of October 25, 1963 makes this interesting statement:

> "There is not even any clear theological reason, much less a legal one, for insisting that Sunday be an official day of rest. It was on the seventh-day, according to the Old Testament, that the Lord rested from the labors of Creation. Nevertheless, Sunday has been the state-decreed day of rest in Christendom ever since A.D. 321, when the Emperor Constantine, a convert to Christianity, decreed that citizens 'shall rest upon the venerable day of the sun.'"

Today it must be reluctantly admitted that the time-honored institution of Sunday, sanctioned by custom, and observed for centuries by Christendom as a sacred day, is not the Sabbath of the Bible, nor is it enjoined in the Ten Commandments. The intrusion of Sunday, no matter how steeped in antiquity, is, as Neander the historian once stated it to be, "always only a human ordinance and it was far....from the early apostolic church to transfer the laws of the Sabbath to Sunday."[43]

How did this change from Sabbath observance take place? Is Sunday observance of God? And does it really make any difference? The historical records of the Christian church in the years immediately following New Testament times are fragmentary, but they are sufficient to make it clear that the change from Sabbath, the seventh-day of the week, to Sunday the first day of the week, was a gradual process.

An Adventure into Discovery

By the fifth century A.D., many Christians were observing both Sabbath (Saturday) and Sunday. Socrates, a church historian of that period, wrote:

> "For although almost all churches throughout the world celebrate the sacred mysteries (The Lord's Supper) on the Sabbath of every week, yet the Christians of Alexandria (in North Africa) and at Rome, on account of some ancient tradition, have ceased to do this."[44]

And Sozomen, a contemporary of Socrates, wrote:

> "The people of Constantinopole, and almost everywhere, assemble together on the Sabbath, as well as on the first day of the week, which custom is never observed at Rome or at Alexandria."[45]

Earlier than that, about the fourth century, a compilation of writings called the *Apostolic Constitutions* instructed Christians to "keep the Sabbath (Saturday), and the Lord's day (Sunday) festival; because the former is the memorial of the creation, and the latter of the resurrection"; and to "let the slaves work five days; but on the Sabbath-day and the Lord's day let them have leisure to go to church for instruction in piety."[46]

Interestingly, none of these writers ever confuse Sunday with the Bible Sabbath. Sunday (the first day of the week), always followed the Sabbath (the seventh day). These records are so clear, in fact, that they help to show us that the weekly cycle, from Christ's time until now, remains unchanged. There is evidence from the third and fourth centuries of Christians keeping the Sabbath in a legalistic Jewish fashion. They met with resistance. Not only then, were people being told to keep both days of the weekend, but there was a controversy regarding how these two days were to be observed. John Chrysostom (died A.D. 407) even goes so far as to say,

> "There are many among us now, who fast on the same day as the Jews, and keep the Sabbath in the same

manner; and we endure it nobly or rather ignobly and basely."⁴⁷

We remember now the *Mishnah* (Jewish rules and regulations compiled about A.D. 200) prohibited the Jews from doing the following "work" on the Sabbath: sowing, plowing, reaping, binding sheaves, threshing, sifting, kneading, baking, writing two letters of the alphabet, tying a knot, tearing in order to sew two stitches, extinguishing a fire, and many more *ad nauseam*.

The Essenes, who hid the Dead Sea Scrolls, were even more rigorous. On the Sabbath nurses were barred from carrying around babies. Nor could a newborn animal, if it happened to fall in a hole, be rescued on the Sabbath. The Sabbath was to be kept in a "spiritual manner," which included "rejoicing in meditation on the law" and attending religious worship services. Paradoxically, as restrictive as the Jews were concerning the Sabbath, they never fasted on that day. Josephus, a first century Jewish historian, insists that not even the noon meal should be skipped.

By contrast Sabbath fasting did creep into the early Christian church. Since Christ was in the tomb on the Sabbath, it was considered by many Christians appropriate to fast on that day. Augustine (died A.D. 430) refers to "the Roman Church and some other churches.... near to it or remote from it" where the Sabbath fast was observed.⁴⁸

As we move back into the second century, we find virtual silence about both Sabbath and Sunday, except for a few references from Rome and Alexandria. Justin Martyr, writing from Rome about the middle of the second century, describes Sunday services in his *Apology*:

> "And on the day called Sunday, all who live in cities or in the country gather together to one place, and the memoirs of the apostles or the writings of the prophets are read."⁴⁹

An Adventure into Discovery

In his *Dialogue with Trypho the Jew*, the same writer grumbled, "Do you see that the elements are not idle, and keep no Sabbaths? Remain as you were born."[50] The so-called Epistle of Barnabus, dated about A.D. 130 and most likely written from Alexandria, notes, "Wherefore, also, we keep the eighth day (Sunday) with joyfulness, the day also on which Jesus rose from the dead."[51] Clement of Alexandria, near the end of the second century, is our first example of a church father who clearly uses the term "Lord's Day" to refer to the weekly Sabbath: "And the Lord's day Plato prophetically speaks of in the tenth book of the *Republic*, in these words: 'And when seven days have passed to each of them in the meadow, on the eighth they are set out and arrive in four days.'"[52]

From these quotations it appears clear that Rome and Alexandria set an early pace in dropping the Bible Sabbath and instituting Sunday in its place. Going back even further into the New Testament itself, what do we find? Jesus, wrote Luke, as He "came to Nazareth, where he had been brought up, "went into the synagogue on the Sabbath day." (Luke 4:16). The women who went to the sepulcher after Christ's crucifixion "returned, and prepared spices and ointments; and rested the Sabbath day according to the commandment." (Luke 23:56). After Christ's resurrection the Apostle Paul attended religious worship services on the Sabbath. (Acts 13:14, 41, 44; 16:13; 17:2, 18:4).

It is interesting that in all these references the New Testament never looks upon observance of the seventh-day of the week as anything other than normal Christian practice. Never, for example, is Paul's attendance at religious worship services on the Sabbath questioned. Rather, it is simply taken for granted. When we consider the strong denunciations against legalism in the New Testament, this fact becomes quite significant. While the matter of Timothy's circumcision was a cause for disagreement (Acts 16:1-3), there was no discord over the keeping of the Sabbath. Since there is no mention of any conflicting opinions, it is apparent that the New Testament apostles recognized only the seventh-day as the Sabbath.

Another striking fact: whereas the apostles are often mentioned as attending religious services on the seventh-day Sabbath in the New Testament, there is no text in the entire New Testament endorsing Sunday sanctity.

Churchman of all faiths concede that Biblical warrant for Sunday observance is lacking. To cite two:

> "There is no word, no hint, in the New Testament about abstaining from work on Sunday…Into the rest of Sunday no divine law enters."[53]

> "The Sabbath is a part of the Decalogue …Until, therefore, it can be shown that the whole moral law has been repealed, the Sabbath will stand….The teaching of Christ confirms the perpetuity of the Sabbath."[54]

What factors, then, led to this gradual change from Sabbath to Sunday? Dr. H. Kunkel says in his Book of the New Testament:

> "The taking over of Sunday by the early Christians is to my mind an exceedingly important symptom that the early church was influenced by a spirit that does not originate in the Gospel, nor in the Old Testament, but in a religious system foreign to it."[55]

Summarily, there were three principle considerations that "influenced" the change. In the first place, Christians in early post-New Testament times looked upon Sunday as a day honoring Christ's resurrection. These Christians, many of whom were Jews, continued the "first-fruits" celebration not as a Jewish festival but in honor of Christ's resurrection. Christ's resurrection is symbolically related to the first fruits of the harvest, just as His death is related to the slaying of the paschal lamb. (See 1 Corinthians 15:20, 5:7) The offering of the wave sheaf (grain sample) of the first-fruits of the harvest was an annual event among the Jews. The habit of keeping the annual first-fruits festival day was transferred into an annual resurrection celebration. It is probable that the weekly Christian Sunday developed later from the annual one. Pope Innocent I (A.D. 402-417) goes on record as giving a reason for the weekly Sunday festival:

> "We celebrate Sunday because of the venerable resurrection of our Lord Jesus Christ, not only at Easter (an annual event) but in actuality by the single weekly cycle (i.e. every Sunday)."[56]

In the second place, anti-Semitism. Jewish revolts, culminating in that of Simon Bar Kochba in A.D. 132-135, aroused Roman antagonism against the Jews and may have caused Christians, especially in the Roman capital itself, to substitute a weekly Sunday to avoid being associated with the Sabbath-keeping Jews. In Alexandria the animosity between Jews and Greeks may have created a similar effect. Both cities are the earliest sites of verified Sunday observance, and both are mentioned by the fifth-century church historians, Socrates and Sozomen, as the two places no longer holding worship services on the seventh day. Capitalizing on the anti-Jewish sentiment, Justin Martyr, writing from Rome in the middle of the second century, presented the most devastating condemnation of the Sabbath. He emptied the day of all its theological meaning, reducing it to a mark that God imposed only on the Jews "to single them out for punishment they so well deserve for their infidelities."

Such a negative view of the Sabbath is reflected in the early introduction of the Sabbath fast by the Church of Rome. The fast was designed not only to express sorrow for Christ's death but also, as Pope Sylvester (A.D. 314-335) emphatically stated, to show "contempt for the Jews—*exsecratione Judaeorum*"—and for their Sabbath "feasting—*destructiones ciborum*." A strict Sabbath fast would naturally preclude also the celebration of the Lord's Supper, since partaking of its elements would be regarded as breaking the fast. Consequently, the Sabbath in Rome was made not only a day of fasting but a day in which no eucharistic celebration and no religious assemblies were allowed.

The Church of Rome appears therefore to have taken concrete measures, on the one hand, to enhance, exclusively, Sunday worship. But why did the Church of Rome pioneer and promote the adoption of the weekly Sunday? A number of factors are worthy of mention. The fact that the Church of Rome—unlike most Eastern churches—was composed of predominantly Gentile converts (Romans 11:13) tended to drive a wedge between the church and the synagogue. It was also in this capital city that Christians were early distinguished from Jews and in order to make that distinction quite clear, the Church of Rome substituted new festivals for characteristic Jewish festivals such as the Sabbath and Passover. Of course, we should also mention the authority exercised by the Bishop of Rome, the only one capable of influencing the rest of Christianity to adopt new liturgical customs such as Easter Sunday, the weekly Sunday, and of course, December 25th as Christmas.

And why was Sunday rather than another weekday such as Friday not chosen to evidence the Christian separation for Judaism? After all wasn't Friday the day of Christ's passion? This brings us to the third major consideration that influenced the change from Sabbath to Sunday—the diffusion of the cult of Mithraism which dominated Rome and other parts of the empire from the early part of the second century A.D. Hutton Webster explains:

> "Early Christians had at first adopted the Jewish seven-day week with its numbered weekdays, but by the close of the third century A.D. this began to give way to the planetary week (Sunday, Monday, Tuesday, etc.); and in the fourth and fifth centuries the pagan designations became generally accepted in the western half of Christendom. The use of the planetary names by Christians attests the growing influence of astrological speculations introduced by converts from paganism....During

these same centuries the spread of Oriental solar worships, especially that of Mithra (Persian sun god), in the Roman world, had already led to the substitution by pagans of dies Solis for dies Saturni, as the first day of the planetary week ....Thus gradually a pagan institution was engrafted on Christianity."[57]

The preeminence that the day of the sun gained over that of Saturn thus apparently oriented Christians toward the same day. It appears likely then, that the choice of Sunday was <u>not</u> motivated by the Christian desire to worship the sun god on its day, but rather by the fact that its symbology adequately commemorated significant divine events, namely, the creation of light and the resurrection of Christ, both of which occurred on the same day. Such a view was carefully expressed by Jerome (A.D. 341-420) when he wrote:

> "If it is called day of the sun by the pagans, we most willingly acknowledge it as such, since it is on this day that the light of the world has appeared and on this day that the Sun of Justice has arisen."

It is easy to understand now why Constantine's first Sunday law used the language familiar to Roman ears, to wit:

> "On the venerable Day of the Sun let the magistrates and people residing in cities rest, and let all workshops be closed. In the country, however, persons engaged in agriculture may freely and lawfully continue their pursuits; because it often happens that another day is not suitable for grain-sowing or for vine-planting; lest by neglecting the proper moment for such operations the bounty of heaven should be lost."[58]

How different this is from the Sabbath law of our Lord, which says nothing of the "venerable" sun, but gives worship to the Creator of the sun.

Following the first civil Sunday law in A.D. 321, Constantine issued another five decrees affecting Sunday observance. From this time forward, both emperors and popes added laws that strengthened Sunday observance. The Roman Catholic church cites the Council of Laodicea as the official voice which transferred the "solemnity from Saturday to Sunday." Note the language of the catechism of Rev. Peter Geiermann, CSSR:

> "Ques.—Which is the Sabbath day?
> "Ans.—Saturday is the Sabbath day.
> "Ques.—Why do we observe Sunday instead of Saturday?
> "Ans.—We observe Sunday instead of Saturday because the Catholic Church in the Council of Laodicea (A.D. 336), transferred the solemnity from Saturday to Sunday."[59]

With each succeeding century that passed, Sunday became more deeply entrenched in the life of the Roman people.

> "In 386, under Gratian, Valentian, and Theodosius, it was decreed that all litigation and business should cease (on Sunday) ....
> "In 425, under Theodosius the Younger, abstinence from theatricals and the circus (on Sunday) was enjoined....
> "In 538, at a council at Orleans, ... it was ordained that everything previously permitted on Sunday should still be lawful; but that work at the plow, or in the vineyard, and cutting, reaping, threshing, tilling, and hedging should be abstained from, that people might more conveniently attend church....
> "About 590 Pope Gregory, in a letter to the Roman people, denounced as the Antichrist those who maintained that work ought not to be done on the seventh day."[60]

With the Roman Catholic Church in the saddle of political and ecclesiastical power, the practice of Sunday observance which she enforced became irreversibly entrenched for more than one thousand year until the Protestant Reformation. Then it was that individuals revolted against religious rites, traditions, and holy days that had supplanted the Word of God for centuries.

Melanchthon, the companion of Luther, was responsible for the final draft of the Augsburg Confession, the most important document of the Reformation, which was signed by the Protestant Princess, and presented in the Diet on June 25, 1530. In it appears the following:

> "Besides these things, there is a controversy whether Bishops or Pastors have the power to introduce ceremonies in the church...They allege the change of the Sabbath into the Lord's Day, contrary as it seemeth, to the Decalogue: and they have no example more in their mouths than the change of the Sabbath. They will needs have the Church's power to be very great, because it hath dispensed with a precept of the Decalogue."[61]

In the 6th century B.C. Daniel the Prophet forecast the rise of just such a power that would "think to change times and laws" (Daniel 7:25). Interestingly, this chapter became the clarion cry of the Reformation. The first sermon that John Knox ever preached was based upon this chapter. Melanchthon, commenting upon this power in Daniel 7:25 charged:

> "They have changed God's laws and turned them into their own tradition to be kept above God's precepts."[62]

In defiance of man-made traditions, many, like some of the Reformers whose conscience were bound by the Word of God, were burnt at the stake because of their faithfulness to divine precepts.

Does it matter today? Is the setting aside of the seventh-day Sabbath of the Ten Commandments in favor of Sunday of concern to God? It is to Jesus. He said, "In vain do they worship me teaching for doctrines the commandments of men." (Matthew 15:9). It's a matter of allegiance: loyalty to God and His Word or loyalty to man and His tradition. Those who persist in the observance of a man-made tradition are obliged to find their warrant in reasons which are equal to God. Ezekiel says we profane the Lord when we profane His day:

> "Her priests have violated my law, and have profaned Mine holy things: they have put no difference between

the holy and profane, neither have they showed difference between the unclean and the clean, and have hid their eyes from My sabbaths, and I am profaned among them....And her prophets have daubed them with untempered mortar, seeing vanity, and divining lies unto them saying, Thus saith the Lord God, when the Lord hath not spoken."—Ezekiel 22:26, 28.

Will His displeasure upon those who profane the Sabbath today be any less than upon those in Ezekiel's time?

In the days of Ptolemy Philadelphus of Egypt, in 284 B.C. there was a celebrated architect named Sostratus, who built a famous lighthouse, all of marble. It was constructed on the island of Pharos, near Alexandria, and its beacon fires kindled every night could be seen by mariners far out to sea. When it was completed, it was greatly admired by Philadelphus, who desired to have his name engraved on the monument for posterity to behold, as the builder. But when Sostratus heard of this scheme, he first engraved his own name on the solid marble, and then covered it with a stucco of mortar, with the inscription, *"Philadelphus, the friend of the gods, and the savior of sailors."*

Time and the elements did their work of erosion, until the inscription bearing the name of Philadelphus was obliterated, exhibiting upon the enduring marble, the name of Sostratus, the original designer. The fabled sanctity of Sunday, the child of mythology, has been plastered over the Sabbath, with the stucco of tradition, and "they have made others to hope that they would confirm the word." But the elements of historical research and Biblical study have eroded the stucco of tradition, revealing the true Sabbath of God and its architect, Christ (Colossians 1:16):

"Remember the Sabbath day, to keep it holy. Six days you shall labor, and do all your work; but the seventh day is a Sabbath to the Lord your God; in it you shall not do any work."—Exodus 20:8-10, RSV.

To believe a "man-made story" or obey God's Word, that's the issue. But there's more, for that obedience to Sabbath rest is a sign of man's total commitment to God. Renouncing the utilitarian use of the one portion, man recognized the sovereign domain of God on the totality. If we love God we are then compelled to cast aside the counterfeit and follow His example of the consecration of Sabbath time (Luke 4:16).

Finally, let it be said that man's life is a measure of time. The use that man makes of his time is indicative of his priorities. We have no time for those toward whom we feel indifferent, but we have time for those we love. The Sabbath rest, then, becomes a test of man's loyalty and love for God. As in human relationships, fellowship can be experienced only by spending time together, so in our relationship with God real communion is possible only when, as Thomas Aquinas said, we *"set aside some time....to vacation with God."* The consecration of the Sabbath time to God is in recognition of His dominion over our life and over the whole creation.

XI
BOOK OF THE DEAD OR WORD OF LIFE

"Brief and powerless is man's life. On him and all his race the slow, sure doom falls pitiless and dark. The life of man is a long march through the night surrounded by invisible foes, tortured by weariness and pain towards a goal that few can hope to reach, and where none may tarry long. One by one as they march, our comrades vanish from our sight seized by the silent orders of omnipotent death."[63]

"Behold me–I have come to you without sin, without guilt, without evil...
I have given bread to the hungry, water to the thirsty, clothing to the naked....
Rescue me; protect me...."

Pleading for eternal life in the judgment hall of Osiris, the dead stood trembling before the forty-two frightful gods who aided the king of the after-life in weighing of souls. One was called "Breaker of Bones;" among his comrades were the "Swallower of Shadows" and the "Eater of Blood." Before them, it was not enough for a man merely to proclaim his own virtue, or to rely on the scarab which had to be placed on his heart to keep it from bearing evil witness against him. He had to know their secret names as well, or else he would be destroyed; he had to be equipped with spells to drive off the snakes and crocodiles who were as dangerous in the afterlife as they were on earth. The proper magic was required to avoid eviction from the sun bark (boat) of the god Re, in which the dead journeyed across the sky; to keep from drinking urine, or forgetting one's own name, or worst of all, dying again in the hereafter.

It was to prepare for these dreadful eventualities that each corpse, usurping a burial custom which once only kings had been privileged to follow, was furnished with a collection of spells, known as the Book of the Dead. Once his tomb contained them, a man was safe, for the spells usually worked; no matter how wicked he actually had been on earth he was promised the rewards of the righteous life.

If the gods decided against him, the book's magic was so powerful that they might even be punished themselves. The journey there was perilous, but if the deceased finally entered the Field of Rushes, life went on as pleasantly as it had in the Nile Valley. Safe in the abode of the blessed, he "plows there and harvests there and drinks there and loves there and does everything he had done on earth."

An illustration from a papyrus *Book of the Dead* found in an Egyptian tomb, pictures the deceased and his wife looking on as the funeral god Anubis weighs the heart of the scribe Ani.

Judgment Scene

The ceremony takes place before the throne of Osiris, in the Hall of Double Justice, while a fierce hybrid monster called the Devourer waits nearby, ready to consume the dead man's heart if it fails to balance with a feather (symbolizing truth) placed on the other scale pan. Such illustrations invariably showed the scales in equilibrium as a token of favorable judgment. After the ibis-headed god Thoth recorded the results and Osiris pronounced his judgment, the deceased enjoyed eternal happiness.

Such as the fate of the ancient Egyptians who, unlike us, accepted and lived with death, and were ready for him. In fact, much of their life was in preparation for eternity. Men of rank spent as much time and care on the preparation of their "eternal homes" as they did on their earthly dwellings, for life is short and death is long. And "home" is a much more accurate description than "tomb" because the Egyptian planned his sepulcher as the everlasting dwelling place of his *"ka"* or spirit.

Book of the Dead or Word of Life

And where did the Egyptian build his "home"? In the West, for that was the home of the dead, and the dead were known as "westerners." In the west the sun-god's boat, having crossed the sky by day, entered upon its nightly journey through the Underworld. Consequently, as in Thebes, nearly all burials were made on the west bank, on the edge of the Western Desert, while the east bank was the home of the living.

Today the east bank of modern Luxor–600 miles south of Cairo–is just a cluster of hotels and villas bordering the Nile. Except for the temples of Luxor and Karnak the east bank of the Nile is drab.

At first glance the west bank seems even less interesting. Yet once upon a time, this uninviting spot supported a large population which served the City of the Dead; there were the quarrymen, masons, plasterers, painters and other craftsmen, who were constantly employed hollowing new tombs out of rock. There were the embalmers, whose workshops stank of embalming fluid, and where corpses lay soaking in baths of natron before being wrapped in strips of linen. There were the morticians whose task was to remove brain, heart and other internal organs, which were then wrapped and mummified separately (thought the heart was usually replaced within the body since it was regarded as the seat of intelligence. Other men were skilled in padding out the sunken flesh over the skull, inserting artificial eyes and generally restoring the corpse to the appearance of life.

There were the makers of funerary furniture–beds, couches, chairs, caskets plated with gold, and the funerary jewelry–golden rings, bracelets, anklets and pectorals–which were placed on the bodies before wrapping. Some of these objects were inlaid with gold and precious or semi-precious stones. And all this wealth was intended to lie forever, deep beneath the rock, in the eternal silence of the tomb; but, despite the desperate stratagem of the priests and architects to preserve the body of the dead, none escaped the wile and cunning of the tomb-robber.

An Adventure into Discovery

Senusrets, Amenhoteps, and Thutmosis suffered the indignity of being tumbled out of their coffins, and their bodies stripped and destroyed. Nonetheless, on the western edge of the Nile, this great industry existed for the sole purpose of preserving and dressing the bodies of the noble dead, and preparing "houses of eternity" for their reception. It has been estimated that some 30 generations of Egyptians were buried in the Necropolis over a period of more than a thousand years.

The Author in the Valley of the Kings

So, my excitement mounted as in the ancient, hired Ford we bumped and swayed along the dusty road towards the Valley of the Kings. At one point we passed the twin statues of Amenhotep III—called by the Greeks the colossi of Memnon—all that is left of the huge temple fronted by these silent giant monuments.

There are pot-holed dirt roads, mud-brick villages and camels. We pass an occasional palm-grove and cotton-field where men, bowed over furrows, use precisely the same primitive hoes which their forefathers used. Barefooted Egyptian girls, veiled in black, pad listlessly along the dusty tracks, balancing water-jars on their heads.

At certain places, eager groups of men in *"gallabiyehs"* rush forward with trays of tourist trash labeled "genuine imitations." The air smells hot and stale and blows sand into one's mouth. Ahead, all one can see is a wall of sun-scorched, arid, fissured limestone cliffs, pitted here and there by black holes.

There is not a single building of distinction to be seen above the ground, apart from the Ramesseum, the funer-

Book of the Dead or Word of Life

ary temple of Ramses II and the temple of Hatshepsut with its successive tiers and columns.

We are approaching the Theban Necropolis where, according to James Baikie, "more wealth, both in sheer bullion and in artistic craftsmanship, was stored away... than in any other spot in the world."

Why did the Egyptian store such fabulous wealth with the dead? It was a part of their religious beliefs. In fact, the custom of burying with the illustrious dead, objects for use in the after-life pervades many ancient cultures. During the Bronze Age, in Asia and Europe, many such burials were made and have been unearthed. But the ancient Egyptians went much further. Not only were their divine kings buried in surrounds of incredible richness and pomp, but even their high officials and noblemen went to the grave accompanied by wealth which was considered adequate for kings in other lands.

Besides wealth, Egyptians painted and sculptured on the walls of their tombs scenes which have no parallel anywhere else in the world–pictures (in the case of non-royal personages) depicting the daily life of the dead man, or if he was a landowner with rich estates, the artists showed his fields and cattle and the workers superintending them. If he was a general he would be shown with his troops; an admiral with his fleet, and even court officials with high-sounding titles such as "Fan-Bearer on the right hand of His Majesty" would be shown hunting wild-fowl in the reed marshes beside the Nile, spearing fish, or presiding over a banquet for their friends. Not only were these scenes faithfully painted, but the scribes wrote above and below them a careful description of the scene, even down to snatches of conversation. The modern strip-cartoon has a history that goes back 5,000 years.

These factors–the mummification of the body, the burial with food, rare and precious things, and the painting on the tomb walls of accurately delineated scenes and inscriptions–not only make Egypt "a superb National

An Adventure into Discovery

Park of ancient life"–but also illustrates one of the most vital aspects of Egyptian religion–that the dead could survive only if the physical body was preserved and supplied with the means of life. Moreover, it was necessary that the body should look as it did in life, so that the spirit "ka" could recognize it and enter into it. Again, it had to be supplied, like a living body, with the necessities of life–food, drink, clothing, and partly be representation in sculpture and painting.

These works of art, though often of a high order, were not created for decoration; they had a magico-religious function–the sculptured or painted replicas became the things themselves. Thus, even if the descendants of the dead man (or priests appointed by them) failed to make regular offerings of food and drink to the "ka," the mere representation on the tomb-walls of cattle, fowl and fields of ripened grain, would be enough to ensure that the spirit would not perish through lack of sustenance.

Also, in this infinitely remote, unearthly, sterile, echoing region of the underworld as hollow as the mountains on the moon were buried forty Pharaohs. Here was Thutmosis I, the first Pharaoh to make his tomb in the valley; Thutmosis II, the warrior; and even Thutmosis III, the "Napoleon of Ancient Egypt", who extended Egypt's dominion from the Sudan to the Euphrates. There are the Amenophises I & II, and the luxury-loving Amenophis III and the nineteenth dynasty conquerors such as Sethi I, Rameses II & III, and Merneptah, and, of course, Tutankhamen.

Due to the failure of the Pyramids to protect the Pharaoh's frail body even though buried beneath thousands of tons of masonry, the Theban hills were chosen as the site for a new kind of tomb. Pharaoh's architects were careful to make the entrances to the tombs as inconspicuous as possible, but beyond that entrance there was a rabbit warren. If the plunderer found it, there were stratagems and puzzles in store for them–blind alleys, elaborately decorated rooms which appeared to be burial chambers, but which were not; behind the decorated walls lay concealed staircases leading down into the rock to the real burial chamber 200 feet below, as in the case of the tomb of Thutmosis I; and always, in the flickering light of the torches, the figures of spirits and demons looking down from the walls.

Today the tomb entrances are either cut in the cliff faces, or approached by flights of stairs descending into the rock. The *ghaffir* (guard) unbolts an iron gate, and one passes from hot sunlight into a dim, cool chamber. A sheet of polished metal is brought to reflect the sunlight into the rock-cut room; the walls suddenly glow with bright colors, as fresh as the day they were applied.

In the mortuary chapel of Sethi I, sculptured in fine relief, eight slim, beautiful girls walk in pairs carrying jars of water to purify the site. Behind them, other maidens perform graceful ceremonial dances symbolizing the re-birth of life on earth. As the light from the ghaffir's mirror trembles on those delicate figures they come alive. Outside the tomb there is nothing but a drab wilderness of dirty sand, littered with broken potsherds; but within the dim chamber the lovely daughters of Pharaoh still dance eternally to his honor. You grope your way into the daylight.

Ahead of the little column of tourists the dragoman in his drab *gallabiyeh*, staff in hand, leads you remorselessly to yet another tomb. Another iron gate swings open; again the dimness after the sunshine; again the sudden flash of mirrored light, again the chattering of voices are hushed into wondering silence.

The dragoman leads his party out of the tomb, and locks the door behind him. You scramble wearily up the sandy slope and see once again the rubbish-heap which was once the City of the Dead, and come away with a sense of sadness. After all, the tombs are empty, which meant in the context of Egyptian religion that the residents of that City had failed in their bid for eternal life.

An Adventure into Discovery

The Royal Valley has ben tidied, with neatly swept paths and iron gates to protect the tombs, and, in spite of the soft-drink stall at the entrance, in spite of the bored taxi drivers dozing in the sun as they wait to take the tourist parties back to Luxor, still the ancient sepulchers of the Pharaohs retain something of their ancient mysteries and terror, but more, they stand as grim reminders of a religion in which the only hope for immortality was in the preservation of a body!

Commenting on the Egyptian philosophy of death, Rawlinson states:

> "Belief in a future life was the main principle of the Egyptian Religion. Immediately after death the soul, it was taught, descended into the lower world (Amenti) and was conducted to the hall of truth, where it was judged in the presence of Osiris....If the good deeds were insufficient, if the scale remained suspended in the air, then the unhappy soul was sentenced, according to the degree of its ill deserts, to go through a round of transmigrations in the bodies of animals more or less unclean."[64]

It is believed that the Greeks received the doctrine of the immortality of the soul from the Egyptians. Commenting on this, the Greek historian Herodotus admits:

> "The Egyptians...were also the first to broach the opinion that the soul of man was immortal, and that when the body dies it enters into the form of an animal, which is born at that moment, thence passing on from one animal to another until it has circled through the forms of all creatures which tenant the earth, the water, and the air, after which it enters again into a human frame and is born anew. The whole period of transmigration is, they say, 3000 years. There are Greek writers, some of later date, who have borrowed this doctrine from the Egyptians, and put it forward as their own."[65]

Plato was the one through whom this doctrine was elaborated and found its way into Christian thought. Dr. J. A. Beet, renowned Wesleyan scholar about the turn of the century gave study to the subject of the immortality of the soul and published his conclusions. After comparing the historic position of the Christian church with the Bible, he said:

> "To sum up. The phrase, the soul immortal, so frequent and conspicuous in the writings of Plato, we have not found in pre-Christian literature outside the influence of Greek philosophy; nor have we found it in Christian literature until the latter part of the second century. We have noticed that all the earliest Christian writers who use this phrase were familiar with the teaching of Plato; and that one of these–Tertullian, expressly refers both phrase and doctrine to him; and that the early Christian writers never support this doctrine by appeals to the Bible, but only by arguments similar to those of Plato....We have failed to find any trace of this doctrine in the Bible....It is altogether alien, both in phrase and thought, to the teaching of Christ and the Apostles."[66]

As Christianity departed from the simplicity of the New Testament, this doctrine of inherent immortality received fuller development. Its complete philosophical elaboration came from St. Thomas Aquinas. Accepting the Aristotelian theory that the soul is the form of the body, Aquinas insisted that, possessing spiritual faculties, intellect and will, the soul was a conscious entity that survived physical death.

Many opposed this non-biblical notion. Martin Luther called it a "monstrous heresy." Jeremy Taylor said, "Immortality is not in his (man's) nature." Archbishop Tillotson in 1690 preached a sermon in which he said: "Immortality of the soul is rather supposed or taken for granted rather than expressly stated in the Bible." A contemporary theologian, Oscar Cullman suggests that it is time the church accepted the hope of the primitive Christians in preference to the views of Plato in this matter. In his famous lecture to the students of Harvard University he said,

> "The concept of death and resurrection is anchored in the Christ-event and hence is incompatible with the Greek belief in immortality....for the first Christians the soul is not intrinsically immortal, but rather became so only through the resurrection of Jesus Christ, and through faith in him."[67]

It is well to remind ourselves of the clear-cut words of Justin Martyr in his Dialogue with Trypho, written after a full century of Christianity:

> "If you have met with some so-called Christians who do not accept this (resurrection) but dare to blaspheme the God of Abraham, the God of Isaac and the God of Jacob who affirm that there is no resurrection of the dead but that when they die their souls are taken up to heaven, do not suppose that they are Christians....But I and any Christians who are orthodox on all points know that there will be a resurrection of the flesh...." (ch. 80)

The idea of the immortal soul as expounded by Plato was accepted in the first century by Philo Judaeus. He was a distinguished Hellenic Jewish writer who was steeped in the spirit and teachings of Plato. His great obsession was to seek to harmonize Jewish religious thought with Greek philosophy. To Philo the body was the source of all evil. It was the coffin or tomb which for a time imprisoned the soul. At death the soul was set free to return to the heavens and enjoy the blessings of the ethereal realms or to descend in misery to the nethermost part of Hades.

James Drummond has summarized Philo's view of the punishment of the wicked thus:

> "Death is not, as men suppose, an end of punishment.... What then, is this death-penalty? It is to live always dying, and to endure, as it were, death deathless and unending."[68]

This belief in the immortality of the soul was not a part of the teaching of the Hebrews and certainly the New Testament does not reflect either the phraseology or thought of Plato. The word *immortality* is found only in 1 Corinthians 15:53, 54, in reference not to the soul, but to the body, which though mortal now will be given immortality at the resurrection; and in 1 Timothy 6:16, *immortality* is spoken of as an attribute of God alone. In contrast to this Plato taught that the soul of man is immortal and imperishable, whereas Christ asserts that the human soul can be destroyed. Jesus in Matthew 10:28 says, "Fear him which is able to destroy both soul and body." A similar thought is found in Matthew 16:25: "Whosoever will save his life shall lose it." The word *destruction*, used frequently in the New Testament to describe the doom of the wicked, is alien to Platonic philosophy.

The words *soul* and *spirit*, so often in modern theological parlance joined with the words *immortal, deathless,* and *never-dying,* come from two words in Hebrew, *nephes* and *ruach*, and two corresponding words in the Greek, *psuche* and *pneuma*. These words are used in the aggregate in the Old and New Testament seventeen hundred times, and yet not once are the terms "immortal," "deathless" or "never-dying" applied to them or to any other terms which would convey the idea of an imperishable nature or continued existence in either the soul or spirit.

The Bible view of the nature of man is that he is a unitary being. When Paul sets forth *pneuma*, or "spirit" in opposition to sarx, or "flesh," he is speaking not of the opposition between two parts of man's being, but of the two directions in which man may travel. The spiritual man is facing toward God and living a life of faith in His salvation. The life in the flesh is that which is apart from God and is headed downward for destruction.

In bringing together the evidence of Scriptural research, in the Old and New Testament, the following summation is presented for consideration:

> The word *mortal* occurs six times in the Bible and in every instance is applied to man. (Job 4:17; Romans

6:12; 8:11; 2 Corinthians 4:11.) The word *immortal* occurs only once in the Bible and is applied to God. (1 Timothy 1:17).

The word *immortality* occurs five times in the Bible and is applied to God or the future state of man beyond the resurrection. (1 Corinthians 15:53, 54; 1 Timothy 6:16; Romans 2:7; 2 Timothy 1:10).

Man can obtain immortality only through Christ. (2 Timothy 1:10; Romans 2:7; 1 John 5:12; 1 Corinthians 15:51-54.)

As indicated previously, the idea of the immortal soul was elaborated by Thomas Aquinas, but was first introduced into the Christian church in the second century by the Greek philosopher Athenagoras. His burden was to show that Christianity and Platonic philosophy were basically in agreement. In his treatise on *The Resurrection of the Dead* he presented an added dimension to Plato's view of the immortality of the soul in claiming man's body assumed its original immortality at the resurrection. Both wicked and righteous reassume this immortal body at this time.

Tertullian, the father of Latin theology, taught the eternal punishment of the wicked. He claimed that the torments of those who are lost will be coexistent with the happiness of the saved.

In Alexandria there was established the New-Platonic school with its most illustrious teacher Origen. This school with its allegorical method of interpreting Scripture did much to undermine faith in the Old and New Testaments. Thus, in the second and third centuries the church lost not only its primitive fervor but its primitive teaching also. Origen's teaching on the preexistence and transmigration of souls and the purifying fires of purgatory appeared time and again in the succeeding centuries and is persistently popular in our own day. Thus, Plato's doctrine on the innate immortality of the soul has been accepted in preference to the conditional immortality as taught in the Old and New Testaments.

Tertullian's teachings of immortality left a lasting impression on later centuries. We see it in the writings of Augustine in the fifth century and in Calvin's teachings in Reformation times. Calvin maintained that in creating man God not only designed to animate a vessel of clay, but He made it the habitation of an immortal spirit.

Notwithstanding these prevailing opinions, voices were raised in defense of the biblical view. One such outstanding example was Sophronius, a learned monk of Damascus who lived in the seventh century and became patriarch of Jerusalem in 634. He taught that man does not possess natural immortality, but that this is a gift of God through Christ; that the condition of man in death is one of unconsciousness (Ecclesiastes 9:5, 6; Psalms 146:3, 4); that all men, good and evil alike, remain in the grave from death to the resurrection (John 5:28, 29). The greatest of the medieval Jewish rabbis, Moses Maimonides, maintained that sinners would perish and the souls of all the wicked would be ultimately extinguished:

> "The punishment which awaits the wicked man is that he will have no part in eternal life, but will die, and be utterly destroyed. He will not live forever, but for his sins he will be cut off, and perish like a brute. It is a death from which there is no return....The reward of the righteous will consist in this, that they will be at bliss and exist in everlasting beatitude; while the retribution of the wicked will be to be deprived of that future life and to be cut off."[69]

John Wycliffe, the morning star of the Reformation in the fourteenth century, denounced the doctrine of purgatory and maintained the unconscious sleep of the dead and that the righteous would receive immortality at the resurrection.

William Tyndale, famous translator of the Bible, declared to his papist opponent:

> "Ye, putting them (departed souls) in heaven, hell and purgatory, destroy the argument wherewith Christ

and Paul prove the resurrection. ... If the souls be in heaven, tell me why they be not in a good case as the angels be? And then what cause is there of the resurrection?"[70]

About a century later, John Milton, author of "Paradise Lost," wrote:

"The death of the body is the loss or extinction of life. The common definition, which supposes it to consist in the separation of soul and body, is inadmissible...For what could be more just, than that he who had sinned in his whole person, should die in his whole person? Or, on the other hand, what could be more absurd than the mind, which is the part principally offending, should escape the threatened death; and that the body alone, to which immortality was equally allotted, before death came into the world by sin, should pay the penalty of sin by undergoing death, though not implicated in transgression?"

Why was the unscriptural doctrine of natural immortality, so acceptable to the ancients, so repugnant to these Reformers? Such a concept of the nature of man teaches the autonomy of sinful man, his independence of God. But the gospel proclaims the reverse–namely man's complete dependence upon God for life and righteousness. The essence of sin is independence of spirit, the feeling that one can get along without one's Maker, and it was to this attitude that Satan lured our first parents when he promised that, by disobedience, they could become as God. (Genesis 3:5, RSV) No wonder then that this false teaching of man's conscious state in death underlies most heathen religions, spiritism, and modern heresies. It is time to return to the Biblical viewpoint.

If, then, Scripture declares that man is a mortal, dependent being, how may immortality become his? Certainly the elaborate ritual, the magic formulas and involved mythology of Egyptian religion are beyond our ken....We're too scientifically minded for this sort of thing–haven't time for superstitious nonsense like boats sailing across the sky and journeys through the nether world. "All that a man hath will he give for his life," records the writer Job, and yet some will surrender even life itself for love's sake. "Greater love hath no man than this, that a man lay down his life for his friends."—John 15:13.

Thus there is one thing, and only one, which is stronger than love of life, and that is love itself. Here is the key to immortality. Our God is love (1 John 4:8, 16). Love is a mightier force than even death, and the love of Christ has "abolished death, and hath brought life and immortality to light through the gospel." (2 Timothy 1:10). Romans 6:23 tells us that "the wages of sin is death; but the gift of God is eternal life through Jesus Christ our Lord."

How is He able to offer us such a gift? Christ "was wounded for our transgressions, he was bruised for our iniquities..." "When thou shalt make his soul an offering for sin..."—Isaiah 53:5, 6, 10, 11) So having satisfied the demands of justice for our sin, Christ went down into the tomb not to be held captive by it, but to destroy its power. Thus he could say, "If a man keep my saying, he shall never see death."—John 8:51. Christ did not mean that a believer, through acceptance of the gospel, would immediately become immortal but rather that the natural death which comes upon all men has for him lost its sting. A believer's faith in Christ renders death as innocuous as "forty winks". Beyond death is the certainty of resurrection and a life that measures with the life of God (1 Corinthians 15:51-55).

We should notice the condition mentioned by Jesus: "If a man keep my saying." The union of the soul with Christ is accomplished by faith, but this union is demonstrated by obedience. He says, "Why call ye me, Lord, Lord, and do not the things which I say?" "If ye know these things, happy are ye if ye do them."—Luke 6:46; John 13:17.

While no soul is saved by obedience, neither can he be saved without it. Obedience testifies to the quality of saving faith. While we are not saved by virtue of our keeping of the commandments, we can certainly be lost forever by willfully breaking them. "For if we sin willfully after that we have received the knowledge of the truth, there remaineth no more sacrifice for sins, but a certain fearful looking for of judgment and fiery indignation."—Hebrews 10:26, 27. It is "he that doeth the will of God" who "abideth forever" (1 John 2:17), for the characteristic of him who has been a partaker of Christ is joyous, wholehearted surrender in all things. Such harmony with heaven's way inevitably results in a life which measures with the life of God.

The disciple who leaned on the bosom of his Lord and who penetrated His thought more than any other has summed up the answer sought by our quest. This is the record, that God hath given to us eternal life, and this life is in his Son. "He that hath the Son hath life, and he that hath not the Son of God hath not life." (1 John 5:11, 12) This is guaranteed by Him who is the Word of Life.

Christianity is not a creed, but a Person. It is not the pursuit of mere outward ritual, but the transformation of the soul by the receiving of the Son of God. To have all else but Him is to have nothing; but to receive Him is to receive all, including eternal life. This Victor over the grave graciously assures each of us that "whosoever believeth in him should not perish, but have eternal life," and He reassures by adding, "Him that cometh to me I will in no wise cast out." (John 3:15; 6:37)

> "Above the ruins of our lives strides the One who today advances that He can authoritatively close the gap between God and man, that He can restore the world deranged by pain, unrighteousness and enmity against God, that He is more than a match for the awful majesty of death."[71]

I believe He is; I really do.

XII
THE LAST DAYS OF POMPEII

> *"The most striking contradiction of our civilization is the fundamental reverence for truth which we profess and the thoroughgoing disregard for it which we practice."*—Vilhjalmuir Stefansson

Long before Rome, Pompeii possessed a stone theater of 5,000 seats, arranged in a semicircle on the Greek model, rising by steps. When Hannibal and his Punic army entered Italy in the third century, this city stood aside, refusing to team up with the cities of Campania which opposed the Romans. On the nearby slopes of the surrounding hills, pasture provided fine and healthy fodder for cattle, so that milk cures were recommended by all physicians, from the great Galen in the second century to Cassiodorus in the sixth century. In fact, the mountain above the town was known as *Mons Lactarius*—"Milk Mountain." Here Oscans, Greeks and Romans lived together peaceably.

It was a favorable site near the sea with everything to be desired, and particularly for the Romans—tub baths, brothels and communal latrines. Nearby was the place where in A.D. 73 the slave rebellion under Spartacus festered in Campania.

Situated in the Bay of Naples, Pompeii was a place of attraction in the ancient world; but this city of luxury and fate was doomed. Toward noon, on February 5, A.D. 63, a fearful earthquake shook the Campanian coast. The tremors rolled like waves from east to west, from Vesuvius toward the sea. The Temple of Jupiter in the forum collapsed. So did the Temple of Apollo—the sanctuary of the Egyptian goddess Isis. One of the city gates fell over, and many dwellings did as well. A fissure in the earth which yawned suddenly in an open field was said to have swallowed up six hundred sheep. The Roman senate un-

An Adventure into Discovery

dertook to repair the damaged city. Nero personally contributed a large sum.

Nevertheless, sixteen years later, when the fearful earthquake was already half-forgotten, tragedy struck, and Pompeii met its appointment with doom! The statue of the Emperor Titus was being raised in the Imperial Temple, and the finishing touches were being put to the work of reconstruction. Then suddenly, in the middle of August in the year A.D. 79, fresh earthquakes shattered the peace of the fruitful region around Vesuvius. The sea grew restless, though no wind was blowing. Cattle and dogs seemed to sense disaster, and a feeling of unbearable tension hung in the air.

Vesuvius had long been considered an extinct volcano. Its slopes were planted almost to its peak with crops and vines, and it was just part of the picture in the Bay of Naples. But the volcano was far from dead. Steam pressure building up inside it had long been seeking an outlet: This pressure had caused the quake of A.D. 63, and had now gathered enough strength to blow Vesuvius sky-high. At its feet lay the twin cities of Pompeii and Herculaneum. August 24, A.D. 79 dawned like any other day in this Roman town and wealthy holiday resort. None dreamed that the sleeping giant one mile away was about to blow its top.

It was lunch time. The shopkeepers had closed for the mid-day siesta. A baker had placed 81 loaves of bread in the oven. A customer had laid his money on the wine shop counter. Then the earthquake came and Vesuvius began its violent eruptions. It was as if God were shaking everyone awake to enable them to escape. The Pompeiians had seen the mountain suddenly split down the middle, its substance rising into the air like a mushroom.

At first the people hoped when the rain began to fall, mingled with ashes and small stones, hoped that the disaster would not directly affect their city, and they sought refuge in their houses and public buildings. This was their doom. The rain did not slacken. It grew steadily heavier.

The Last Days of Pompeii

Lapilli (volcanic stones) as large as eggs and larger, mingled with fine dust and ashes, fell upon the entire city for three days, building up on the roofs until these collapsed under the weight. Streets, squares and interior courtyards were soon covered. The rain water and ash together formed a clinging mud that impeded movement. A good many citizens were wise enough to jump on their horses and make a get-away. Some called for their slaves and if these in their terror did not come quickly enough, they themselves hitched up the mules, placed wife and children in the wagon and headed for the open country.

In the mud-coated streets many fugitives slipped, fell and could not rise again. At the gates of the city, vehicles piled up; people had to clamber over the bodies of fallen horses. Walls collapsed, pillars crashed to the ground. Everywhere tiles slid from the roofs, the dust and ashes obscured the vision, the torrents of rain extinguished the lamps. Nevertheless, the only safe place to be was in the open. A great many people did not realize this in time.

Children who had been playing in the gardens sought shelter under the roof overhangs until the roof collapsed, burying them. Women hastened to their living quarters to gather a few articles of value; men weighed themselves down with purses of money and precious household gear. The form of one man was found lying in the street; he was still clutching his jewels and coins. But they did not save him. Slaves tended to their sick masters; doorkeepers would not leave their posts—all perished. Some lingered to save precious possessions. Others spent priceless moments loading carts with their treasures, only to be caught in the circle of death. Those who sought the shelter of basements and solid vaulted cellars did not grasp the nature of their danger. The fine dust crept through every crack and sulfurous fumes suffocated the unfortunates.

With fire belching from Vesuvius and the ashes raining from the sky, with the populace stricken by horror, a Jew remembered the destruction of cities recorded in the book of Genesis, *"Then the Lord rained brimstone and fire* on Sodom and Gomorrah, from the Lord out of the heavens." (Gen. 19:24, NKJ) That disaster had been a punishment for the sinfulness of the people. Was God again punishing the unbelievers as He had punished them once before? So the Jew, remembering the names of those cities, whose doom should have been a warning to all ages, wrote on the wall of a house in the ninth district of the city in which he was trapped, the words: SODOMGOMORA.

Thirty-four people and one goat died in the lower chambers of one of the most elegant villas of Pompeii, just beyond the walls of the city. The master of the house was evidently heading for the garden gate with a sack full of gold coins, perhaps to see whether escape toward the sea was still possible. Death struck him at the threshold of the house, together with the slaves who were carrying the household's silver utensils. Two convicts in a dungeon cell, who had not been released from their leg irons, perished as wretchedly as the chained watchdogs in the houses.

Those who escaped the doomed city via the Western Gate, hurried toward the sea, anxiously seeking a ship. But most of the ships had already lifted anchor and were now far out to sea, fighting for life, for the earthquakes had raised towering waves. Those which remained—cargo vessels and fishing boats, even the last leaky rowboat—were crowded with fugitives. They tried to push off from the shore and were held back by those who desperately hoped to wedge themselves in, until at last the boats sank under their burden or were swallowed up in the raging surf. People, dogs and rats had plunged in blind terror into the water, hoping to swim to safety. Their bodies were washed up on the beach. Dead fish and birds lay among them on the sand. Seeing the doom by the seashore, some people tried to make their way back to the city. But they could not get through the steady stream of fugitives and wandered about on the beach until their strength gave out.

The Last Days of Pompeii

In a tomb on the highway that led to Herculaneum, a family had gathered for a funeral when the rain began. The people were lying on the couches set out in the anteroom of the burial vault, about to begin the funeral supper. Perhaps they did not think it right to cut short the ceremony immediately, and before they could finish, it was too late. Suffocated in the tomb, they followed the newly deceased member of the family into death.

Back in the fated city, not even Isis could safeguard her priests; one of them died in the street, having delayed his flight to collect a sackful of religious utensils, sacrificial vessels and coins. Two other priests of Isis fled from the temple on the old triangular forum; they were felled by collapsing columns. Others died inside the temple itself. The crash of falling buildings and the patter of falling stones drowned out the cries of the dying. Darkness shrouded the city.

When Vesuvius quieted down on the morning of the third day, when the wind scattered the clouds and the sun broke through once more, white ashes fifteen to twenty feet deep lay like funeral shroud over the city and its environs. Two thousand lay dead.

Pompeii lay under a blanket of death for seventeen centuries, till in 1748 a peasant found some remarkable statues beneath his vineyards. Since then the site has been excavated and the tragic story revealed. The forms of several Roman sentries were found at the eight city gates where they had remained motionless at their posts amidst the crashing elements. In the museum in the present-day excavated Pompeii you can see the forms of a girl lying face down; a dog whose limbs were twisted in grotesque shapes showing the agony of its last moments, and that of a man crouched in a corner with arms and hands up as though to shield his face from the grim death that awaited him. In one of the chambers of the temple was found a huge skeleton with an axe beside it; two walls had been pierced by the axe—the victim could penetrate no further.

An Adventure into Discovery

Death came suddenly to Pompeii. The shops never opened after that fateful noon hour, the barmaid never picked up the money off the counter, carts laden with possessions still block the city streets, and as I walked the streets of Pompeii I saw the possible answer as to why the tragedy was allowed. The evidence still remains to show that Pompeii was a veritable Sodom and Gomorrah—a center of moral corruption. The walls of Pompeii today still carry the widely known phallic symbols pointing the way to practitioners of the oldest profession; and behind many of the endless locked gates lie concealed Pompeiian pornography that the present day guides delight in showing to visitors, sometimes for a price. Statues in the museum reveal the sadly perverted and sex-obsessed condition of the people of that time, which is aptly described by Paul in his letter to the Romans where he declares that those who practice such vice deserve death (ch. 1:24-34).

The ruins of Pompeii with Mt. Vesuvius in the background

Paul's dark picture of corruption can be verified from the secular writings of the first century. Seneca, a contemporary of Paul, declares:

> "Every place is full of crime and vice; too many crimes are committed to be cured by any possible restraint. Men struggle in a mighty rivalry of wickedness. Every day the desire for wronging is greater, the dread of it less; all regard for what is better and more just is banished; lust hurls itself wherever it likes, and crimes are now no longer covert. They stalk before our very eyes, and wickedness has come to such a public state, has gained such power over the hearts of all, that innocence is not rare—it is non-existent."[72]

The Last Days of Pompeii

As I walked the streets of Pompeii and later read these words of Seneca, I was stunned with the parallel between Pompeiian and 20th century morals. An astute observer of America's sex scene and former professor of sociology at Harvard University, Dr. P. A. Sorokin, says:

> "There has been a growing preoccupation of our writers with the social sewers, the broken homes of disloyal parents and unloved children, the bedroom of the prostitute, a cannery row brothel, a den of criminals, a ward of the insane, a club of dishonest politicians, a street-corner gang of teenager delinquents, a hate-laden prison, a crime-ridden waterfront, the courtroom of a dishonest judge, the sex adventures of urbanized cavemen and rapists, the loves of adulterers and fornicators, of masochists, sadists, mistresses, playboys. Juicy lovers, id, orgasms, and libidos are seductively prepared and served with all the trimmings."

Who can doubt that this world, like Pompeii, is ripe for the fiery judgment of God? Paul leaves no doubt as to the destiny of those "who knowing the judgment of God commit "fornication, wickedness, covetousness, maliciousness...murder...deceit, malignity...inventors of evil things, disobedient to parents...without natural affection..." for "they which commit such things are worthy of death" (Romans 1:29-32). The certainty of a day of accountability being further reinforced by the author of the book of Hebrews who wrote, "It is appointed unto man once to die and after that the judgment" (ch. 9:27). The same writer warns "It is a fearful thing to fall into the hands of the living God" (Hebrews 10:31).

The reading of this verse reminds us of the sermon on this text preached by the great American revivalist, Jonathan Edwards, at Enfield, Massachusetts, July 8, 1741. In this sermon Mr. Edwards graphically pictured the solemn day when sinners will be called to account for their rebellious lives. So effective was the presentation that as the audience listened they felt drawn into the immediate presence of God. Judgment day seems to be upon them. One writer, in describing the occasion, said that there was "such a breathing of distress" that the evangelist was compelled to stop and urge the people to regain their composure. So real were the descriptions of "Sinners in the Hands of an Angry God" (the title of the sermon) that the listeners thought at any moment they would hear the last trump sound.

Of course intellectual defenders of the Christian faith ridicule such preaching as "unpurified Christian temper"[73] and argue God's love should be stressed, not His anger. The problem is that God's love has been emphasized and misrepresented to the extent that men have almost lost sight of the judgment. Certainly God *is* love, but His is *also* a consuming fire. He *is* love, but He also exercises a holy wrath against which nothing can stand." Behold, the day of the Lord cometh," urges an Old Testament prophet, "cruel both with wrath and fierce anger...and he shall destroy the sinners thereof out of it" (Isaiah 13:9).

It is useless to attribute this solely to the coming judgment on the Israel of that day. God continues to work in the same way, and this warning can well include the world of today. For us, the word of Habakkuk remains valid: "O Lord...in wrath remember mercy." The loving forgiveness of God is just as real as His wrath; His love and mercy are as available as His judgment is certain. Paul had no illusions about the matter. "But you have a hard and stubborn heart, and so you are making your own punishment even greater on the day when God's anger and righteous judgments will be revealed. For God will reward every person according to what he has done" (Romans 2:5, 6, GNB). Later in the same letter Paul says: "By His death we are now put right with God; how much more then, will we be saved by Him from God's anger" (ch. 5:9).

A brief survey of the Bible indicates that there will be a final, irrevocable separation between believers and unbelievers that consigns one group to a place of comfort, and the other to a place of vengeance (cf. Matthew 25:46

and Revelation 20:15). Significantly, whenever judgment is mentioned, it is always coupled with salvation. The destruction of the ungodly is linked at the same time with the rescue of the saints (e.g. Revelation 19:1-8); but before this final, executive phase of the judgment, a hearing, an investigation of each one's life occurs. A scrutiny so detailed that "every idle word that men shall speak" will be judged (Matthew 12:36), for "God shall bring every work into judgment, with every secret thing, whether it be good, or whether it be evil"—Ecclesiastes 12:14. According to the Scriptures, this hearing will precede Christ's return. In Revelation 22:12, Jesus says: "Behold, I come quickly; and my reward is with me, to give every man according as his work shall be." If Christ brings His reward with Him, this suggests that there is a pre-advent judgment.

Further, Jesus in the parable of the two harvests (Matthew 13:24-30) confirms that a judgment takes place before His return. Two harvests are set forth: (1) the harvest of the righteous, typified by the wheat, and (2) the harvest of the wicked, set forth in the symbol of the weeds. Jesus says that the weeds must be bound and burned and the wheat is gathered in. But how and when will the wheat and weeds be distinguished? Obviously *before* the harvest. And when is the harvest? Jesus answers, "The harvest is the end of the world" (Matthew 13:39). The work of distinguishing wheat and weeds precedes the harvest. When the work of distinguishing and investigating is done, the proclamation of the harvest is issued from heave, "Thrust in thy sickle and gather" (Revelation 14:15). Rewards are distributed.

One of the most remarkable Scriptures that clearly indicate a judgment before Christ returns is Revelation 14:6, 7. These verses contain a special message that is to prepare men for the coming of Christ. Of this message John writes, "I saw another angel fly in the midst of heaven, having the everlasting gospel to preach unto them that dwell on the earth, and to every nation, and kindred, and tongue, and people, saying with a loud voice, Fear

God, and give glory to him; for the hour of his judgment is *come*: and worship him that made heaven and earth, and the sea, and the fountains of waters."

In the first century, when the Apostle Paul was on trial before the Roman governor Felix, he called Felix's attention to the "judgment to come" (Acts 24:25). In the apostle's day the judgment was yet future. Not so today when the return of Christ is imminent. Today God's message is, "The hour of his judgment is come." The judgment work is now going forward in heaven, and when every case has been considered, Jesus will come to reward the faithful. "For the son of man shall come in the glory of his Faith with his angels; and then he shall reward every man according to his works" (Matthew 16:27).

Daniel had a vivid preview of this pre-advent judgment when he wrote: "I beheld till the thrones were cast down, and the Ancient of days did sit, whose garment was white as snow, and the hair of his head like the pure wool: his throne was like the fiery flame...thousand thousands ministered unto him, and ten thousand times ten thousand stood before him: the judgment was set, and the books were opened" (Daniel 7:9, 10). According to the Psalmist, "God (the Ancient of days) is judge himself" (Psalms 50:6). The thousands upon thousands who stand in God's presence and assist in the judgment are undoubtedly the angels. These are the representatives of the heavenly government who "always behold the face of my Father which is in heaven" (Matthew 18:10). Because God the judge, and the angels as witnesses in the judgment, one other figure takes a prominent part—Jesus Christ. Daniel writes, "I saw in the night visions, and behold, one like the Son of man came with the clouds of heaven, and came to the Ancient of days, and they brought him near before him" (Daniel 7:13).

As the judgment begins in heaven, Christ the Son of man is brought near before God. What is Christ's role? What part does He play in this judgment that decides human destiny? The answer is, Jesus is our attorney; He is our mediator. "We have an *advocate* with the Father, Jesus Christ the righteous" (1 John 2:1). "There is one Mediator between God and men, the man Christ Jesus" (1 Timothy 2:5). A further dimension of His role in the pre-advent judgment is symbolized in the Old Testament sanctuary service. Leviticus 16 describes the service known as the "Day of Atonement" (or *Yom Kippur*). It was a special annual service during which the High Priest entered the Most Holy Place alone in order to ceremonially cleanse the sanctuary of the sins of the people which had accumulated there in the course of the year.

Each day the sins of the people by way of the blood of the sacrifices were transferred into the sanctuary, and once a year the sanctuary was "cleansed" by the removal of sin. The High Priest officiated in the place where the ark, the mercy seat and the brilliant presence of God could be seen. Only if all the sins of the people were repented of could the High Priest emerge from that shining presence of God alive. Paul says that since the cross "we have a great High Priest who has gone into the very presence of God—Jesus, the Son of God" (Hebrews 4:14, *GNB*) for us. Unless Jesus Christ can demonstrate that the righteous have *all* been forgiven justifiably, that God not only can but has the right to forgive their sins, the righteous cannot be saved.

This pre-advent judgment, then, is both a judgment of the people, and it is also a judgment involving the Priest, for He enters that veil as their representative. "For Christ did not go into a man-made Holy Place…He went into heaven itself, where He now appears on our behalf in the presence of God" (Hebrews 9:24 *GNB*). Another passage that hints at this enormous dimension of the plan of salvation is Daniel 8:14 which reads, "And unto two thousand, three hundred days, then shall the sanctuary be cleansed."

In the preceding chapter VII we noted the 70-week time prophecy of Daniel 9:24-27. Both of these prophecies are related because the 70-week prophecy is *"cut off"*

An Adventure into Discovery

the longer time period mentioned in Daniel 8:14. Therefore, both of these periods begin at the same time. The striking fulfillment of all the events prophesied in the sort 70-week time period sets the seal on the chronological outline of Daniel 8:14. This passage in Daniel indicates that an important phase of the judgment began in 1844, at the end of the 2300-day prophecy. Remember Revelation 14: "The hour of his judgment is *come*." This message announces something happening *now*. Just as the earthly sanctuary was "cleansed" by the removal of sin, so, according to Daniel's prophecy, the heavenly sanctuary was to be "cleansed" from the record of man's sin. Paul, interpreting the significance of the sanctuary in the New Testament context, confirms this when he states, "It was therefore necessary that the patterns of things in the heavens should be purified (cleansed) with these; but the heavenly things themselves with better sacrifices than these" (Hebrews 9:23). In other words, the "cleansing" of this record of man's sin will not be affected by the blood of animals, but by the blood of Christ.

As the cleansing of the heavenly sanctuary involves *judgment* and an *investigation* of the records of men. So, in this judgment God is showing the whole universe that His way with each person who claims His forgiveness is fair and just. He does this to free us from suspicion and to show that we can be trusted with eternal life. In this judgment the truth will be told. Our mistakes and sins will not keep us out. The records in heaven will show that they have been forgiven by the blood of Jesus Christ. Like the plaintiff in a civil case, we need to take our case to court with Christ s our defense attorney. Our advocate is more than willing to represent us.

What then should be our response? Living in this crucial judgment hour time, what must we do? Paul focuses on the alternatives we have. "Some men's sins are open beforehand, going before in judgment; and some men they follow after" (1 Timothy 5:24). The alternatives are atonement or judgment. Sins which are "open beforehand" can be confessed and forgiven. "If we confess our sins, He is faithful and just to forgive us our sins and cleanse us from all unrighteousness" (1 John 1:9). "I even I, am he that blotteth out the transgressions for mine own sakes, and will not remember thy sins" (Isaiah 43:25). But sins unconfessed remain on the record and appear against us in the judgment. If we don't permit Christ to bear the "iniquity of us all" then we will bear the responsibility for our own sins. Calvary was God's way of teaching the world what would have happened to it, if it had been left to itself. "The wages of sin is death" (Romans 3:23).

One of the strangest cases of jurisprudence in American history was the case of George Wilson. Wilson robbed a mail train near Reading, Pennsylvania, in 1829. He was apprehended, convicted and sentenced to die for his crime. One June 14, 1830, President Andrew Jackson granted Wilson a pardon. However, since Wilson hated Jackson and his politics, he refused to accept the pardon. The judicial system now faced a dilemma. Should a pardon be forced upon him? The Supreme Court reviewed the case. Their decision was stated as follows:

> "A pardon is a deed to the validity of which delivery is essential, and delivery is not complete without acceptance. It may be rejected by the person to whom it is tendered; and if it be rejected, we have discovered no power in a court to force it to him."

George Wilson went to his death because he refused a presidential pardon. Paul assures man that "by the free gift of God's grace all are put right with him through Christ Jesus, who sets them free. God offered Him, so that by His death He should become the means by which people's sins are forgiven through their faith in Him" (Romans 3:24-26, GNB).

On the porch of an old house in England is this inscription cut in stone, *Cadenti porrigo dextram*—"I stretch out my right hand to him that is falling." All men have fallen. All men have been forgiven. Like George Wilson, we are free to accept the provision that will give us life.

An Adventure into Discovery

The hand of God is stretched toward us caressingly. God is "just and the justifier of him that hath faith in Jesus." Is it more than a problem of the intellect to us? Has it wrought itself out in our heart and life? "He is able to save them to the uttermost that come unto God by him, seeing he ever liveth to make intercession for them" (Hebrews 7:25).

WHAT THEN?

"When the plants of our mighty cities
Have turned out their last finished work;
When our merchants have sold their last yardage
And have dismissed the last tired clerk,
When our banks have raked in their last dollar
And paid out their last dividend;
When the Judge of the earth says, *"Closed for the night,"*
And asks for a balance—WHAT THEN?

When the choir has sung its last anthem,
And the preacher has made his last prayer,
When the people have heard their last sermon
And the sound has died out on the air;
When the Bible lies closed on the altar,
And the pews are all empty of men,
And each one stands facing his record
And the Great Book is opened—WHAT THEN?

When the actors have played their last drama,
And the mimic has made his last pun;
When the film has flashed its last picture,
And the scoreboard displayed its last run,
When the crowds seeking pleasure
Have vanished and gone out in the darkness again,
When the trumpet of the Ages has sounded,
And we stand up before Him—WHAT THEN?
    —*Selected*

XIII

THE GOLDEN AGE: A NEW BEGINNING

> *"I know there are utopians who believe that human progress is inevitable, a divine trajectory irreversible in its upward motion. Let me just point out to them that in the last few thousand years we have blazed what I consider to be a trail of questionable glory— from Abraham and Isaac to Dennis the Menace."*
> –Adlai E. Stevenson

Malcolm Muggeridge, addressing the International Congress on World Evangelization at Lausanne, Switzerland, gloomily remarked: *"It has long seemed to me clear beyond any shadow of doubt that what is still called Western Civilization is in an advanced stage of decomposition, and that another Dark Age will soon be upon us. If, indeed, it has not already begun."*

Others, applying evolution in a cheerful sort of way conclude, to the contrary, that limitless advancement is due to the working of a universal law and will continue until the state we call perfection is reached.

> "Progress is therefore not an accident but a necessity. As surely as a blacksmith's arm grows large and the skin of a laborer's hand becomes thick, as surely must the things we call evil and immortality disappear so surely must man become perfect."

Science, we are led to believe is the golden key to nature. "It is not", said Sir James Frazer, "too much to say that the hope of progress, moral and intellectual as well as material, in the future is bound up with the fortunes of science." The uninterrupted advance of science and technology seem to suggest that heaven is just around the corner. To these optimists, material improvements promise faster travel, bigger cities, better plumbing, a more abundant diet, wealth for all. There is even a case to be argued for moral progress; after all, slavery has been abolished, human life is valued and there are sound reasons to conclude that the human race is healthier and happier than ever before.

Evolution has provided a "scientific" explanation of the way progress takes place, and made progress clearly inevitable; improvement is just as real as gravity. In case we are inclined to think that such a rosy-tinted view is simply 21st century optimism, we should note that the prophets of progress are still around crying "peace and plenty"–despite two devastating world wars and the disintegration of society. The dream that somehow biological evolution and human progress are the one and same thing, continues to allure. Few writers have achieved as wide and respected a reading public as Pierre Teilhard de Chardin. By presenting an evolutionary mystique, de Chardin suggests "that the universe has direction…resulting in some sort of perfection. Hence some belief in progress."[74]

Others try to be realistic about present trends. For example, Gordon Wolstendholme says:

> "Advances in the sciences are doubling accumulated information every ten years. As the experts contemplate the future, they are disturbed by the potentialities of evil that might arise from the application of their findings. Already biological research is in a ferment, creating and promising methods of interference with natural processes which could destroy or transform nearly every aspect of human life which we value."[75]

We are confronted, then with two conflicting pictures of life–progress and regress; a universe that is getting better and a universe that is becoming worse; evolution and devolution; growth and decay. Dazzled by the technological achievements of the nineteen and twentieth centuries, we have overlooked the fact that ancient cultures associated the golden age with the past, not the future. The dazzlingly beautiful new Babylon which was built by Nebuchadnezzar was resurrected from the memory of such illustrious forbearers as Hammurabi and Sargon.

The Golden Age: A New Beginning

These men were real giants, and controlled large empires that were wisely administered and effectively governed. Hammurabi's famous Code of Laws issued:

> "To cause justice to prevail in the country
> To destroy the wicked and the evil
> That the strong may not oppress the weak."

This is an outstanding example of judicial enlightenment and comes "surprisingly close to our modern ideas of justice".[76]

The monuments, palaces, temples and private houses from this period are of outstanding quality. Mesopotamian society in the eighteenth and nineteenth centuries B.C. was quite sophisticated; education was of a high standard; writing, religion, history and mathematics were taught, and advanced skills were practiced.

Five hundred years earlier, Sargon of Akkad made such an impression on the world that his personality became surrounded with the everlasting halo of legend. Sargon's sphere of influence stretched from Afghanistan to Lebanon, from southern Russia to the Indian Ocean. Securing necessary supplies of timber and precious metals, he was able to raise the standard of living to an exceptionally high level.

We can trace the same conviction that the best days belong to the past in Egyptian, Roman and Greek thought. All the glories of Egypt's New Kingdom failed to surpass those of the Twelfth Dynasty. For 206 years art flourished; pyramids were built; the Faiyum was brought under cultivation. Nubia was conquered; trading expeditions were sent to Somaliland, Crete and Asia Minor; smiths developed high standards of technical expertise. Yet always something better seems to have happened before: The peak of Greek culture was attained under Pericles, not Alexander the Great; Rome, great though it was, had been preceded by the Etruscans; the Myceneans were indebted to the Minoans; and back at the dawn of human history, the shadow of the Egyptian Old Kingdom and the magnificent Sumerians.

The name Cheops, Kephren and Mycerinus are immortalized in the stone of the pyramids of Giza. Sparse though the information is that comes to us from this period, it is sufficient to convey some idea of the kind of spirit that animated man at the time of his greatest achievements. The economic and cultural life of 2,500 B.C. staggers us with its accomplishments, and dazzles us with its splendor. Nothing can match the genius of Imhotep. Here is a man who is able to construct mountains of stone out of massive blocks weighing about two and a half tons each. Built in courses rising stepwise from base to peak, the step pyramid towers hundred of feet into the air. The same Imhotep is a wise sage, an accomplished physician, and a politician in his own right. No wonder the Egyptians deified him.

Under Cheops, pyramid building was perfected to such an extent that it is without parallel anywhere in architecture. The orientation of the Great Pyramid is phenomenally accurate. The four sides are aligned almost exactly on north, south, east and west. The maximum error is only one twelfth to one twentieth of a degree. One wonders what ancient engineer could lay out this great structure with such precision. How was it done? The fineness of workmanship is almost beyond belief. Using bronze saws with jeweled cutting points, Egyptian stone cutters were able to cut to within a hundredth of an inch from a straight line. Using

A Pyramid in Giza, Egypt

The Golden Age: A New Beginning

no machinery other than the lever, 16-ton blocks were maneuvered into position and jointed together as closely as one five-hundredth of an inch.

Yet at the same time as the Egyptian Old Kingdom was flourishing, the civilization of Sumeria radiated over the entire Near East, and exerted a powerful influence on all succeeding cultures. The great archaeologist, S. N. Kramer, is convinced that Sumer is where history begins; and at its beginning are refined City States, highly developed agricultural communities, water conservation, intricate irrigation systems; literature, commerce, bookkeeping... the lot. "Far from being primitive, the Sumerian Society of Early Dynastic times was thoroughly organized, one is even tempted to say over-organized. The Sumerians were meticulous people with bureaucratic minds."[77] The huge state machinery that was set up by these industrious people was as complex as anything the welfare state has ever devised. From their records we are able to discover that they operated a sort of Guild or Trade Union System. There were separate shepherds for male and female asses, separate groups of fishermen according to whether they fished in fresh, brackish or sea water; even snake charmers had their own organization. Merchants, artisans, scribes, controllers, inspectors, overseers, and other officials were listed in much the same way as in the yellow pages of the Telephone Directory.

Apparently the progression from simple to complex is not as clear in human affairs as it seemed to those who thought that the theory of evolution could be applied in every area of life. Civilizations do not appear to have evolved at all. We have no reason to conclude that we are progressing towards the perfect State; quite the contrary may be the case. The more one looks at history and legend, the more one is tempted to think that man may have reached the zenith of his powers in the past rather than the present or the future; even the Sumerians imagined there had been better days, and that there was a far-off land in their remote past more wonderful than Lagash and more prosperous than Eridu. In the myth of

"Enki and Ninurta",[78] there is mention of a pure, clean and bright land where death, disease and sorrow were unknown.

> "*The raven utters no cries*
> *The ittidu-bird utters not the cry of the ittidu-bird*
>   *The lion kills not*
> *The wolf snatches not the lamb*
>   *Unknown is the kid-devouring dog."*

This wonderland is called Dilmun, a country which is usually associated with Bahrain on the Persian Gulf; but without being specific, the legend could possibly reflect the biblical story of a lost Paradise. The Sumerians also believed that their ancestor, Adapa, lost his right to immortality. The list of Sumerian kings contains dynasties of supermen who lived for thousands of years. Alongside these ancients, the biblical Methuselah was a mere boy. The first two kings of Eridu, for instance, are supposed to have reigned for 64,800 years.

Whatever we make of these myths, the point is obvious: the idea of man evolving into a perfect being and creating a heaven for himself on earth is comparatively recent. As long as Judaeo-Christian traditions were accepted with their talk of sin and their story of the Fall of Man, and of man being turned out of his Eden home, there wasn't much chance of us fooling ourselves into thinking that we were the greatest. The memory of Eve's mistake and the forbidden fruit kept us humble. Adam's failure reminded us that we are only shadows of what we once were. We have absolutely nothing to brag about. Paradise was lost and it is not in our power to regain it without Divine help.

In any case, what right have we to conclude that growth is something that can go on and on and on without ceasing? As a matter of fact, growth is bound by rigorous laws from which there is no escape. The plant develops, flowers and dies. The child becomes a man and when he reaches maturity, growth ceases and he dies. The pattern is obvious:

The Golden Age: A New Beginning

"Man born of a woman is short-lived and full of disquiet
He blossoms like a flower, and then he withers
He slips away like a shadow and does not stay!
He is like a wine stain that perishes
Or a garment that moths have eaten."—Job 14:1, 2

The second law of thermodynamics states that our world is running down towards disorder and entropy. Yet in spite of this, we assume that at the same time complex and highly ordered systems have been evolving and will continue to do so, *ad-infinitum*. The fact is that the strength of a system depends upon the raw materials that are needed to maintain its growth level. In the past, successful civilizations were able to guarantee supplies because they lived off the interest and not the capital of their resources. The American Indians lived off the buffalo herds without ever depleting them. The use of non-renewable resources was minimal; but modern man has been eating into capital at such a rate that soon essential resources will be exhausted and the entire economic system will grind to a halt.

We have mined the earth to its bottom. We have taken more out of the soil than we have put in. Yields are beginning to decline, in some cases very substantially. Intensive farming has overstocked land; intensive cultivation has produced erosion. No part of the earth is self-sufficient in all critical minerals. It has been estimated that by 2042 commercial deposits of silver, tin, uranium, natural gas and crude oil will be running out. If consumption increases at its present rate, the United States will then require four and one half times the amount of metal and energy it now uses. And if world demands reach the present per capita level of the United States, they will be thirty times greater. What will happen when the industrial nations can no longer lay their hands on the vital raw materials that are essential for their existence? Already energy demands exceed population growth by 100%.[79]

The world already faces a serious water shortage. Water is essential to industry and the quantities that are used are staggering. It takes 4,400 gallons of water to make a ton of steel; 350 gallons to make one gallon of beer; 800 gallons to make a ton of cement and 20,000 gallons to make 1 ton of paper. While a man in developing countries manages on 2 gallons per day, a Londoner requires 33 gallons for domestic use and an American's demand amounts to 55 gallons. It seems inconceivable that the most common commodity there is could be drying up; but as man advances his thirst for water rockets. Engineers estimate that in the decades to follow the United States will consume one third of all the water flowing into its rivers and lakes, for cooling.

All the evidence tends to show that the idea of progress is an illusion. Indeed, it can be shown that the very things we associate with progress have, in fact, contributed to regress. The world has already passed its peak and is now running out of steam. We put chemicals and artificial fertilizers into the soil only to discover that they have impoverished it. We damn rivers in the hope of increasing the area of arable land only to find that productivity has in many cases decreased through salinization. We invent plastics and manufacture indestructible wastes.

Professor Barry Commoner, director for the Center of Natural Biology at Washington University, states unequivocally:

> "Never before in the history of this planet has its thin life-supporting surface been subjected to such diverse, novel, and potent agents. I believe that the cumulative effects of these pollutants, their interactions and amplification, can be fatal to the complex fabric of the biosphere. And, because man is, after all, a dependent part of this system, I believe that continued pollution of the earth, if unchecked, will eventually destroy the fitness of this planet as a place for human life."[81]

There's more. We crowd together in cities and lose our peculiar identity; at the same time we destroy the essential structure of society by severing the bonds that tie individuals into families and families into communities.

The Golden Age: A New Beginning

With modern medical techniques we keep tired hearts beating and diseased lungs breathing and over-worked kidneys functioning only to ensure the survival of the unfittest.

All this is done in the name of progress. But the idea of limitless progress is more, much more of a myth than dreams of a past golden age and a lost paradise ever were. The memories of Dilmun, and a Garden of Eden, and an angel with a flaming sword and a foolish woman eating forbidden fruit and falling from grace, are far more realistic than the vain hopes of egotistic man. The limits of economic and demographic growth have already been reached and so have the limits of growth in natural systems. Terrible chaos lies ahead unless the industrial nations turn their back on their policies of unlimited growth and expansion. Says a chorus of informed opinion.

> "Like lemmings, man is heading for the far bank of the river. Suicide is not his intention. Has he the intelligence to turn back? The lesson of history is that he never avoids catastrophes; he just spends his time recovering from them. No doubt history will repeat itself."[82]

Perhaps our obsession with the notion of progressive evolution is our undoing.

> "The present blind faith in progress and in the power of a growing national product are obviously leading us to a dead-end...And soon there will be no going back; for man will have sold himself out."[83]

As far as progress is concerned the end of evolution has already been reached. The Bible was right all along. It was never optimistic of man's attempts at self perfection. From Genesis to Revelation, it views human history as devolution, not evolution. From the heights of Eden, man descends rapidly into a "bottomless pit." Deprived of his god-hood, he nevertheless aspires to be like God and tries to achieve divinity by scientific and technological means.

An Adventure into Discovery

> *"You thought in your own mind,*
> *I will scale the heavens*
> *I will set my throne above the stars of God*
> *I will sit on the mountains where the gods meet*
> *In the far recesses of the north*
> *I will rise above the cloud-banks*
> *And make myself like the Most High*
> *Yet you shall be brought down to Sheol (grave)*
> *to the depths of the abyss."*—Isaiah 14:13-15.

The only way for man to go forward is to go back to the beginning and start all over again. That is the theme on which the New Testament ends.

> "Then I saw a new heaven and a new earth; for the first heaven and the first earth had vanished, and there was no longer any sea. I saw the holy city and new Jerusalem, coming down out of heaven from God–I heard a loud voice proclaiming from the throne 'Now at last God has his dwelling among men. He will dwell among them and they shall be his people; and God himself shall be with them. And he who sat on the throne said, 'Behold I am making all things new.'"–Revelation 21:1-4.

Here is an integrated community, a social structure based on sound principles, with the prospects of stability, growth and genuine progress. The heavenly city comes down from above; it isn't something that man erects himself. It is the result of supernatural, not natural processes. It doesn't evolve. "For it is by grace you are saved; it is not your own doing. It is God's gift. There is nothing to boast of."—Ephesians 2:8, 9.

This gift will be a renovated earth, not a "palace in the sky." This is why the Bible opens and closes with a description of a new earth. The former tells of this world in the beauty of pristine perfection; the latter pictures this fair estate freed from every vestige of suffering and decay and all the things that grieve the human spirit. One was the dwelling place of our first parents before sin entered; the other will be the one of the righteous after sin has been forever put away. The wise man declared: "Behold the righteous shall be recompensed on the earth"—*Proverbs* 11:31. Christ himself positively confirmed this hope when he promised: "The meek shall inherit the earth."—Matthew 5:5. Peter vividly describes that from the ashes of this planet and human failure a glorious new earth will arise:

> "That day will bring about the destruction of the heavens by fire and the elements will melt in the heat. But in keeping with His promise we are looking forward to a new heaven and a new earth, the home of righteousness." –2 Peter 3:12-13.

This new beginning calls for an environment that will correspond with God's original plan for earth.

> "The desert and the parched land will be glad; the wilderness will rejoice and bloom. Like the crocus, it will burst into bloom; it will rejoice greatly and shout for joy...Water will gush forth in the wilderness and streams in the desert. The burning sand will become a pool, the thirsty ground bubbling springs....No lion will be there, nor will any ferocious beast get up on it; they will not be found there. But only the redeemed will walk there, and the ransomed of the Lord will return. They will enter Zion with singing; everlasting joy will crown their heads. Gladness and joy will overtake them, and sorrow and sighing will flee away."–Isaiah 35:1, 2, 6, 7, 9-10.

A renovated earth will be inhabited by regenerated man, "For the perishable must clothe itself with the imperishable, and the mortal with immortality"—1 Corinthians 15:53. "Then will the eyes of the blind be opened and the ears of the deaf unstopped. Then will the lame leap like a deer, and the tongue of the dumb shout for joy..."—Isaiah 35:5, 6.

Do you begin to realize what this will mean to us? We will throw away our glasses and see with perfect, undimmed vision. We will cast aside our crutches, our canes, our wheelchairs... our hearing aids, artificial limbs. Crippling arthritis will no longer burn into aching limbs; no more cancer wards or heart disease. Pious imagination! The musings and daydreams of those who sigh for the "beautiful isle of somewhere"? No. "Strengthen the feeble hands, steady the knees that give away; say to those with fearful hearts, 'Be strong, do not fear; your God will come...he will come to save you.'"–Isaiah 35:4.

There is more, much more. "He will wipe every tear from their eyes. There will be no more death or mourning or crying or pain, for the old order of things is passed away"—Revelation 21:4. Neither accident, nor disease, nor old age will terminate life. The heart-break of gazing into the face of a dying loved one and choking out a last agonizing "good-bye" will be unknown.

What will these ageless inhabitants of the "golden age" do? They will be engaged in the erection and occupation of houses, pursuing pleasurable horticultural pastimes; they will experience satisfying labor with permanent enjoyment.

> "Behold, I will create new heavens and a new earth. The former things will not be remembered, nor will they come to mind...They will build houses and dwell in them; they will plant vineyards and eat their fruit. No longer will they build houses and others live in them, or plant and others eat. For as the days of a tree, so will be the days of my people; my chosen ones will long enjoy the work of their hands...they will be blessed by the Lord..." –Isaiah 65:17, 21-23.

In this world, most labor hard for a lifetime and reach the age of retirement too old, too sick and too tired to reap the dividend of life's investment; but in the golden age of this new beginning "the inhabitant shall not say, I am sick." (Isaiah 33:24). Think of the unlimited capacity for achievement. Today we are frustrated by our limitations. Our minds far outstrip the capacities of our abilities. "The spirit is willing but the flesh is weak;" but there:

> "Every faculty will be developed, every capacity increased. The acquirement of knowledge will not weary

The Golden Age: A New Beginning

the mind or exhaust the energies. There the grandest enterprises will be carried forward, the loftiest aspirations reached, the highest ambitions realized; and still there will arise new heights to surmount, new wonders to admire, new truths to comprehend, fresh objects to call forth the powers of mind and soul and body."[84]

That will be real progress in an unending existence from which a friend never went away.

We are approaching the climax of the human drama when time is about to merge into eternity and history will become a part of infinity. There the future will always be the present. The laser light of Scripture cuts through the gloom of our tormented age and promises hope. As William L. Lawrence reflected,

> "Yet the sound of the swinging keys need not necessarily mean closing time for man at the twilight of his day on this planet. It could also mean the opening of gates at a new dawn, to a new earth–and a new heaven."[85]

I was in London. I strolled into Trafalgar square and up the stone steps of the Tate Gallery. I wanted to view for myself George Frederic Watts famous painting bearing the caption "Hope". It is unforgettable and moving. A beautiful, blindfolded figure sits on a globe which represents the world. The girl holds in her hand a harp, all the strings of which are broken–all except one. In the dark, grey sky above there is just one star. With her hand, the blindfolded girl is touching the one string, and her lovely head is bent toward it in closest attention, earnestly waiting to catch the note of that one vibrating wire. So Sir Frederic Watts conceived of hope triumphant over failure, sorrow, pain and death. After seeing this famous painting, Harold Bigby wrote these lines:

> *"And ever on her lonely string*
> *Expects some music from above,*
> *Some faint confirming whispering*
>   *Of fatherhood and love;*
> *One star, one string, and through the drift*
>   *Of aeons and with human cries,*

An Adventure into Discovery

*She waits the hand of God to lift
The bandage from her eyes."*

Soon the Infinite God will lift the bandage from our eyes. Man's today will be succeeded by God's tomorrow. So:

> "...Think of Stepping on shore and finding it Heaven!
> of taking hold of a hand and finding it God's hand,
> of breathing new air and finding it celestial air,
> of feeling invigorated and finding it immortality,
> of passing from storm and tempest to an unknown calm
> of waking up and finding it Home!"
> —from Finally Home by L. E. Singer

Our *Adventure Into Discovery* is over, but a new beginning has just started. Our wish for a life with meaning is a reality and the extension of that life eternally, a promise. It has been pointed out the wish for immortality is an evidence of its reality. C.S. Lewis maintains that it would be strange for a man to hunger for something that did not exist. So, our longing for immortality is a "race memory" of something once seen–when men lived by centuries and but for sin might have lived forever–but now invisible.

In the story of Faust, the aged philosopher, having neglected God, disillusioned, curses life, which for him is almost gone. The devil appears to him and offers him renewed youth in exchange for his soul. That this story was used as the base for a play by Marlowe, a poem by Goethe, and an opera by Gounod, is no accident. It expresses an answer to a universal wish.

The wandering Jew, according to legend, struck Christ and said, "Hurry up," as He was carrying the cross on the way to Golgotha. As punishment, he was not allowed to die, and his youth was renewed each hundred years. Here again myth expresses a universal wish. It can be more than a wish for "... *the youth* (who) *will die at the age of one hundred*" (Isaiah 65:20). This wish will come true!

ENDNOTES

1. Ellen G. White, *Education*, (Pacific Press, 1952), 173.

2. Wil Durant, *The Story of Civilization*, Vol. VI.

3. See William H. Shea, "Two Palestinian Segments From the Eblaite Geographical Atlas" in *The Word of the Lord Shall Go Forth*, pp. 606–610. Published for the American Schools of Oriental Research by Eisenbrauns, Winona Lake, Indiana. 1983.

4. Nelson Glueck, *Rivers in the Desert*, Philadelphia: The Jewish Publications Society of America, 1969.

5. W. F. Albright, *The Old Testament and Modern Study*, p. 25.

6. Professor Frank M. Cross, "Christian Century" (Aug. 11, 1955), p. 920.

7. Dr. A. T. Pierson, *Many Infallible Proofs*, pp. 30, 31.

8. See Daniel 7:1; 8:20, 21; Luke 2:1; Matthew 22:17–21; John 11:48; 19:12; Acts 25:10).

9. Flavius Josephus, *Antiquities*, Book 10, chap. 11.

10. *Gaudiumetspes*, par. 80.

11. "The Urge to Self-Destruction", *The Observer*, Sept. 28, 1969.

12. Bertrand Russell, *The Sunday Times*, Nov. 10, 1957.

13. Frank Baumer, *Religion and the Rise of Skepticism*, p. 67.

14. *Tacitus Histories*, Vol. 13

15. John Dowling, *History of Romanism*, pp. 541, 542.

16. Abraham Davenport, *Connecticut Historical Reflections*, p. 403.

17. *American Oracle of Liberty*, Vol. X, No. 472.

18. Charles P. Snow, *Time*, November 11, 1974. p. 76.

19. *Christian Century*, July 7, 1965.

20. See Lewis M. Simons, "Weapons of Mass Destruction" in *National Geographic*, November 2002, pp. 2–35.

21. William Vogt, *Road to Survival*, p. 78.

22. "Nuclear War: The Long View", *Newsweek*, November 7, 1983.

23. Dr. Carl Sagan, *Parade Magazine*, October 30, 1983, p. 7.

24. E. O. Jones, *Christianity and other Religions*, p. 115.

25. Cyril Eastwood, *Life and Thought in the Ancient World*, p. 34.

26. Jacquetta Hawkes, *Man and the Sun*, pp. 125–162.

27. Lenormant, *Manual of the Ancient History of the Near East*, Vol. 11, p. 219.

28. See Geza Vermes, *The Dead Sea Scrolls in English*, Penguin 1968, p. 46.

29. *The Works of Flavius Josephus*, "The Wars of the Jews", Vol. I. Trans. William Whiston, (Baker, 1977).

30. *Standards of Morality* (Mowbray, 1967), p. 36.

31. H. Maryon, "The Colossus of Rhodes", *Journal of Hellenic Studies*, Vol. LXXVI, 1956.

32. Ellen G. White, *Education*, p. 250.

33. *De Specialibus Legibus*, 11, 60 (Loeb Classics, Philo, VII).

34. *Ethica Nicomachea* X, 6.

The Golden Age: A New Beginning

35. Rabbi Solomo Alkabez, *Lechah Dodi*.

36. D. M. Canright, *The Morality of the Sabbath*, pp. 26, 27.

37. P. Massi, *La Domenica*, p. 376.

38. Henry Law, *Christ Is All*, p. 101.

39. *Exposition of the Epistle to the Romans*, p. 699.

40. William Shakespeare, *Merchant of Venice*, Act III. Sc. 2.

41. Robin Fedden, *Syria*.

42. Leonard Cottrell, *One Man's Journey*.

43. August Neander, *Neander's Church History*, First Ed. Vol. 1, p. 339.

44. Socrates, *Ecclesiastical History*, v. 22.

45. Sozomen, *Ecclesiastical History*, vii. 19.

46. vii. 23 and viii. 33 Trans. *Ante-Nicene Fathers*, Vol. VII, pp. 469–495.

47. John Chrysostom, *Commentary on Galatians*, cited from *Nicene and post Nicene Fathers*, Vol. XIII, p. 8.

48. Augustine, *Epistle 36*, par. 27. *NPNF*, 1st series, Vol. 1, p. 268.

49. Justin Martyr, I. ch 67, *ANF*, Vol. I, p. 186.

50. Justin Martyr, ch. 33, *ANF*, Vol. 1, p. 206.

51. ch. 15, *ANF*, Vol. 1, p. 147.

52. *Miscellanies*, v. 14 ANF, Vol. 11, p. 469.

53. Canon Eyton, *The Ten Commandments*, pp. 52, 63, 65.

54. T. C. Blake, D.D., *Theology Condensed*, pp. 474, 475.

55. H. Kunkel, *Versteendis Des Neue Testament*, p. 76.

56. Pope Innocent I, *Epistola*, 25.7.

57. Hutton Webster, *Rest Days*, pp. 220, 221.

58. Eusebius, *Life of Constantine*, Bk. 1, Ch. 32.

59. Peter Geiermann, *The Convert's Catechism of Catholic Doctrine*, p. 50, 2nd ed., 1910.

60. James T. Ringgold, *The Law of Sunday*, pp. 265–267.

61. *Of Ecclesiastical Power*, Pt. 2, art. 7.

62. *Exposicion of Daniel the Prophete*, British Museum Library.

63. Bertrand Russell, *Mysticism and Logic*, p. 56.

64. Henry C. Rawlinson, *Ancient Religions*.

65. Bk. 2, ch. 123 (Trans. G. Rawlinson).

66. *The Immortality of the Soul*, pp. 53, 54.

67. Oscar Cullman, *Immortality and Resurrection*, pp. 9, 11.

68. James Drummond, *Philo Judaeus*, Vol. II, pp. 33.

69. Quoted in Edward White, *Life in Christ*, p. 222.

70. See Tyndale's Preface to the New Testament, ed. 1534.

71. Helmut Thielicke, *The Silence of God*.

72. *Moral Essays*, I, 183.

73. Friedrich Schleiermacher, *The Christian Faith*, p. 716.

74. Teilhard de Chardin, *The Phenomenon of Man*, p. 284.

75. Gordon Wolstendholme, *Man and his Future*.
76. George Roux, *Ancient Iraq*, Pelican 1969, p. 186.

77. Roux, op. cit. p. 124.

78. S. N. Kramer, *Suermian Mythology*, pp. 54–59.

79. See Hugh Montefiore, *Can Man Survive*.

80. *National Geographic*, September, 2002, p. 2.

81. Barry Commoner, *Science and Survival*, p. 122.

82. G. R. Taylor, *The Doomsday Book*, p. 305.

83. Edwards Goldsmith, *Can Britain Survive*, 1971, p. 135.

84. Ellen G. White, *The Great Controversy*, p. 677.

85. William L. Lawrence, *The Hell Bomb*, p. 147.

We invite you to view the complete
selection of titles we publish at:
www.TEACHServices.com

scan with your mobile
device to go directly
to our website

Please write or email us your praises, reactions, or
thoughts about this or any other book we publish at:

P.O. Box 954
Ringgold, GA 30736

Info@TEACHServices.com

TEACH Services, Inc., titles may be purchased in bulk
for educational, business, fund-raising, or sales
promotional use. For information, please e-mail:

BulkSales@TEACHServices.com

Finally if you are interested in seeing
your own book in print, please contact us at

publishing@TEACHServices.com

We would be happy to review your manuscript for free.

www.ingramcontent.com/pod-product-compliance
Lightning Source LLC
Chambersburg PA
CBHW070535170426
43200CB00011B/2431